BULLY-PROOFING YOUR SCHOOL:
Teacher's Manual and Lesson Plans

Carla Garrity, Ph.D.   Kathryn Jens, Ph.D.   William Porter, Ph.D.

Nancy Sager, M.A.   Cam Short-Camilli, L.C.S.W.

Published and Distributed by

SOPRIS
WEST™
EDUCATIONAL SERVICES

A Cambium Learning™ Company

4093 Specialty Place ◆ Longmont, Colorado 80504 ◆ (303) 651-2829
www.sopriswest.com

Acknowledgments

We would like to thank the board and administration of the Cherry Creek (CO) School District for the opportunity to develop the *Bully-Proofing* program. We are grateful for their continued commitment to educational excellence and to developing a safe school climate where teachers can teach and students can learn.

The program presented in this book was supported in part by funding from Nancy and Sam Gary, as well as from the Rose Community and Cherry Creek Schools Foundations. This financial support allowed us to continue to develop, research, and refine our safe school program and present the third edition of our work. With the professional efforts of Dr. Vicki Meyer, Paul Von Essen, and our training team, we were able to reach hundreds of schools across the country to promote safe schools. Drs. Larry Epstein and Amy Plog spearheaded the research component of our program and helped develop the assessment tools, including the Colorado School Climate Survey.

Finally, we want to thank the many students who have demonstrated a commitment to having their schools safe for all students. All of them have taught us so much and have inspired our continued effort to create safe schools for everyone.

About the Authors

Carla Garrity, Ph.D., practices child psychology at the Neuro-Developmental Center, a multi-disciplinary group for the assessment and treatment of children. She has worked for over 25 years developing preventative programs for the well-being of children. For many years, Carla supervised and taught at the University of Denver's School of Professional Psychology. The author of numerous books in the field of children and divorce, she developed an interest in recent years in children victimized by bullies. Working with colleagues in the Cherry Creek (CO) School District, she developed *Bully-Proofing Your School*. She also co-authored a companion book, *Bully-Proofing Your Child: A Parent's Guide*.

Kathryn Jens, Ph.D., works as a psychologist in the Cherry Creek (CO) School District and has an independent practice with a specialization in psychological trauma. She completed her graduate study of clinical-community psychology at the State University of New York at Buffalo in 1978.

After years of working with crime victims, Kathryn is particularly excited about this project for its preventative possibilities. As a result of this project, she has also developed an interest in the moral development of children and in intervention with children exhibiting antisocial personality patterns.

As a single parent, she is grateful to her four children for their input, their patience with her busy life, and for their courageous efforts to stop bullying.

William Porter, Ph.D., received his doctorate in child clinical psychology in 1978 from the University of Denver and has devoted his professional career to developing mental health programming for children and families. He worked in community mental health for Denver (CO) General Hospital prior to joining the Cherry Creek School District, where he has directed a wide variety of student programs for more than 25 years. Bill has been instrumental in developing outdoor therapeutic, suicide prevention, home alone, adolescent runaway, violence prevention, and a number of other intervention programs. He believes in using every possible opportunity to reach a child or family, and his program efforts have received local and national acclaim. Bill is a co-author of *Bully-Proofing Your Child: A Parent's Guide*.

Nancy Sager, M.A., is an Education and Behavior Consultant with the Cherry Creek (CO) School District. She has worked with special needs children for over 30 years. She believes the Bully-Proofing program provides a level of support to children that broadens their repertoire of skills necessary for success today as well as in the future.

Nancy wishes to thank her husband, Don Ruggles, for his encouragement and unending support.

Cam Short-Camilli, L.C.S.W., has been a school social worker with the Cherry Creek (CO) School District for the past 14 years. She has worked at both the elementary and middle school levels. She received her B.S.W. from Western Michigan University and her M.S.W. from Michigan State University. Cam's interest in bully-victim problems developed around concerns that students and parents brought to her. She has continued to learn from using this program and listening to students.

Cam wishes to thank her husband and two sons for their tremendous support on this project.

Contents

List of Handouts and Transparencies

Preface

Aggressive behavior in students has long been a disruptive element in the educational arena. At a time when violence is so prevalent in our society, bullies have become a (sometimes lethal) threat to the physical and emotional safety of students. Many of us can probably recall personal or professional experiences with bullies. The recall of these memories is intense and awakens strong emotions, especially of fear and helplessness. The pervasiveness of the fear results in a feeling of powerlessness. Bullies bring this imbalance of power and fear to schools, as well. After suffering unchecked bullying, self-destructive acts or desperate retaliation with lethal weapons is not uncommon.

A most discouraging situation is occurring in many schools today. Many children are unwilling to turn to staff for help with bullying because they believe that not only will the staff fail to help them but that telling will make the situation worse. Although we as educators would like to believe that we can simply send children to handle these problems on their own, many need adult support to develop the coping skills necessary to protect themselves from the attack of bullies. The old adage "Just hit 'em back" is one of the myriad of unsuccessful myths surrounding bullying behavior and is in fact probably one of the most dangerous strategies with a true bully. However, there are many approaches that can defuse the situation and lower the potential for aggression. For instance, just having more adults among students has been shown to influence bullying behavior.

Eighty-five percent of the students in schools are neither bullies nor victims. This "caring majority" of students, though, observe the behavior and interactions of bullies, live with an uncomfortable feeling about their own safety, and often believe that if they get involved the aggressive actions will be transferred to them. Fear and power struggles are a reality in elementary schools, and one of the goals within schools must be to bring these issues in line so they are manageable. The actions and influence of this caring majority are a powerful resource with which to maintain the value of kindness and decency. They are the untapped reservoir of strength, the leverage for impacting change in creating a safe school environment for all children.

The *Bully-Proofing Your School* program operates on many levels within a school. It is our belief that developing the caring majority's intervention skills so they feel confident to be involved is crucial. Their power is implicit by number, and explicit by positive acts of kindness toward victims. By developing a strong, reinforced identity, they can help set the tone of a school and dictate its operating environment. This group can give strength and support to the victims and defuse the power of the bullies.

Bullies can occupy an inordinate amount of time from staff, students, and parents. Swift and precise adult interventions that avoid power positions and clearly establish bullying behaviors as unacceptable can prevent the wounds of repeated victimization. Escalating direct power struggles with bullies is exhausting and generally not effective. Intervening calmly and consistently before bullying behavior escalates can strip the bully's power.

Many standard curriculum packages fail after three to four months because there is an expectation inherent to them that all staff members can and will intervene in the same manner. A lack of congruence between an individual and curriculum can cause the program to be undermined—one becomes uncomfortable with the new way and thus returns to one's old style. However, this will not be the case with this program. We strongly believe, and have designed this program around this tenet, that the acknowledgment of personal styles up front is crucial in formulating a team ethic comprised of multiple approaches achieving the same goal. Teachers need to identify and accept the skills they already have that can be implemented in a focused fashion to impact aggressive behavior, support the strength of the caring majority, and soothe the wounds of victims. The wheel doesn't need to be reinvented, just to be mounted and balanced.

The community should also be included in recognizing and supporting a "no-bullying" position. Addressing bullying behavior requires strong support from parents to prevent fractionalizing of the community. Understanding some basic tenets, such as that all parents believe their children are the victims and that very rarely are children self-confessed bullies, helps clarify the picture and enables collaborative relationships with parents to stop bullying.

Developing a comprehensive approach will lead to successful results in identifying and intervening with bullies. As a supplement to the *Administrator's Guide to Staff Development* and the *Teacher's Manual and Lesson Plans* this book presents two curriculums designed to be used in individual or small group formats: one for interviewing with bullies, the other for understanding and supporting the victims. These activities focus on kindness and inclusion for all students, and when used in conjunction with the rest of the *Bully-Proofing Your School* curriculum will help change the balance of power within a school.

Why Bully-Proof?

Scope of the Problem

In the average elementary school classroom, two to three students spend their day afraid. Some of these children avoid the restroom, cafeteria, and playground because they fear they will be humiliated or picked on by bullies. The United States Department of Justice and the National Association of School Psychologists (NASP) estimate that 160,000 children miss school each day because of fear (Lee, 1993).

Increasingly, children simply do not feel safe at school—safe from violence, safe from humiliation, and safe from bullying. Every seven minutes bullying happens on elementary school playgrounds (Pepler, 1998). Children as young as second grade report that no one helps them; they do not believe that their teachers or the other school staff will help protect them if they report their fear. Indeed, research confirms that what these children are reporting is true. Most of the time no one helps and, if anyone does, it is more likely to be another child than an adult.

Consequently, children are left feeling helpless, afraid, and "on their own" to figure out how to cope with these feelings. Many younger children hide throughout the school day, experience physical symptoms of distress, or even refuse to attend school. As they grow older, children are more likely to take more active measures to protect themselves—often these are not positive measures. Some will begin carrying weapons to school, others will associate with a gang for protection, and still others will drop out of school entirely.

Every day approximately 100,000 children carry guns to school. As many as 6,250 teachers are threatened each day, and of those about 260 are actually attacked (Lee, 1993). School violence is multidetermined and not solely the result of bullying. However, what is bullying behavior in elementary school can easily turn into violence by middle and high school.

The *Bully-Proofing Your School* program can be an early, preventative measure against this type of behavior. More importantly, however, it is designed to stop bullying at the elementary level to ensure a safer school environment—one that does not tolerate acts of physical or emotional aggression against children. It is within this type of safe and caring environment that children can learn. And it is within your influence to provide just such an environment.

The *Bully-Proofing Your School* Program

Bully-Proofing Your School provides a blueprint for an elementary school to easily implement a bully-proofing program designed to meet one criterion: to make the school environment safe for children both physically and psychologically.

Bully-Proofing Your School encompasses a number of underlying principles:

▶ **It is the responsibility of adults to ensure that school is a safe environment in which children can learn.**

Many children live with fear every day at school. This can be incapacitating and can severely affect learning.

The participation of the staff is an important element in the success of the *Bully-Proofing* program.

▶ **Bullies, when confronted with a caring community (a unified group of adults and peers within a school), are defused.**

This program enables the "caring majority" (the majority of students who are neither bullies nor victims) to intervene and thus strip the bullies of their power.

▶ **Bullying is not synonymous with conflict.**

Bullying takes many forms, and school staff must be able to discern between bullying and conflict.

▶ **The *Bully-Proofing* program will be most successful if implemented comprehensively.**

While the program is somewhat flexible in order to embrace the varying levels of resources from school to school, it will have limited success if implemented piecemeal. Each component of the program is as important as any of the others—it is their combination within a school that will coalesce into a safe learning environment.

▶ **Punitive programs are only successful with bullying behavior to a point.**

Bully-Proofing Your School is not a punitive program. Rather than engaging in power struggles by attempting to discipline bullies, this program focuses on shifting the power away from the bullies.

▶ **There are many means to any end.**

Positive training can change the atmosphere of the school. The power of the caring majority can help to make the school a safe learning environment. It can also promote character development and skills for becoming a responsible community member.

This program emphasizes the importance of recognizing and utilizing the different styles, strengths, and experience of the staff members. Each individual role is significant, and each contributes to the successful implementation of the bully-proofing program, establishing a positive and safe environment for all.

The *Bully-Proofing Your School: Teacher's Manual and Lesson Plans* Contents

Bully-Proofing Your School: Teacher's Manual and Lesson Plans presents both a process and all the materials necessary for the teacher's portion of the school-wide program against bullying. The program is easy to implement and maintain, and flexible in terms of the time required. If consecutive weekly lessons are presented to the students, the entire program can be completed within a two to three month time frame from start to finish.

The sequence of this *Teacher's Manual* is as follows:

▶ **Chapter One: Defining Bullying**

This chapter defines the bullying behavior that will be addressed by the program and identifies specific forms which that behavior takes. Also described are the characteristics of both bullies and victims and the dynamics of their relationship within a school.

▶ **Chapter Two: Intervention in Bullying Situations**

This chapter makes the case for the necessity of adults to intervene in bullying situations and provides guidelines for situations requiring adult intervention. A handy "Developmental Guide to Conflict Resolution" is also provided for quick reference.

▶ **Chapter Three: Student Instruction**

This chapter provides a complete classroom curriculum to educate all students about bullying and what they can do about bullying occurring around them. Role play, modeling, class discussion, and classroom materials (posters, etc.) are utilized to teach students specific strategies and techniques to cope with and prevent bullying behavior.

The curriculum consists of eight weekly sessions with an additional follow-up session, but is meant to be used flexibly to conform to the demands of individual classroom schedules. The classroom curriculum has activities and instructions specified for grades K–6.

▶ **Chapter Four: Creating and Maintaining the Caring Majority**

This chapter provides specific techniques for shaping the climate of the school into a safe, respectful, and inclusive environment. Intervention skills for changing the silent majority of children into a caring majority are described. The caring majority provides strength and support to the victims and defuses the power of the bullies. This is the most powerful resource in creating a safe and caring school environment.

▶ **Chapter Five: Collaboration With Parents**

This chapter details methods for effectively communicating with the parents of both bullies and victims to ensure collaborative relationships between the school and home.

▶ **Resource Guide**

Recommended resources on topics such as collaboration, discipline, conflict resolution, coping skills, and assertiveness are referenced throughout the chapters.

Chapter One
Defining Bullying

All children are the victims of occasional teasing behavior or aggression, but some children are repeatedly targeted. True bullying is **repeated exposure** over time to negative actions. Bullying means there is an **imbalance of power** so that the child being victimized has trouble defending himself or herself. Bullying is aggression. It can take many forms, including physical, verbal, or psychological. **Bullying** is when one person uses power in a willful manner with the aim of hurting another individual repeatedly.

Normal Peer Conflict — What Bullying Is Not

Conflict is an inevitable part of interaction. As children learn the give and take of friendship, of group cooperation, and of social interaction, conflict naturally occurs. Social skills are developmental. Children gain greater capacity for empathy, for compromise, and for kindness to others as they mature cognitively and emotionally. Children in the early elementary years (grades K–2) do not always think of others. Their goal in both friendship and play is egocentric, or self-centered. They pick playmates in order to have a good time and to maximize their own excitement. They believe that a good friend is one who will do what they want. A common response to frustration is one of rejecting the other child. A first grader might say, for example, "If you won't play house with me, I won't invite you to my birthday party."

By the middle elementary grades, children gradually begin to understand friendship and play as a process that involves fun for all participants. Games with rules begin, recess time is spent with others who enjoy the same interests and activities, and sharing is seen. Still, children of this age do not fully understand or engage in mutuality or compromise. Play is fun when everyone gets their needs met, but conflict erupts when access to things or frustration of needs occurs. The capacity to listen to and understand another person's point of view is still not fully developed and only the most mature of children will employ compromise to solve problems during grades 2–4.

By the later elementary grades, children evolve gradually toward a consideration of others. Feelings and personal needs are shared. Having secrets and sharing them through notes and private plans is common. Friendships become exclusive and cliques form. Jealousy and feeling left out are common problems. Mutuality, commitment, and loyalty are hallmarks of social interaction. At this age, compromise is a skill that can be taught and used to solve problems.

Normal peer conflict is typically characterized by the developmental level of the children involved. Aggression and hurtful remarks are part of conflict at all ages; they do not necessarily mean that a bully-victim problem exists. Bullying can be recognized by the following unique social interactional features:

- Bullying is repetitive negative actions targeted at a specific victim.

- Bullying is an imbalance of power so that the victim has trouble defending himself or herself. This imbalance can be the result of physical size or the result of emotional or cognitive capacity. Overall, the critical feature is that

DEFINITION

Bullying is when one person uses power in a willful manner with the aim of hurting another individual repeatedly.

the victim does not have the skills to cope.

 ▶ Bullying is usually characterized by unequal levels of affect. The child being victimized is typically very upset. This may be manifested by withdrawal, outright crying and anguish, or anger. Regardless of the specific behavior observed, the content and process is one of extraordinary distress on the part of the victim. The child doing the bullying, on the other hand, is typically devoid of affect. He or she is likely to show little outward emotion and to communicate through words or action that the victim provoked or deserved the aggression. Little or no empathy or caring for the victim is evident. The child who bullies feels justified in his or her actions.

Table 1 highlights the main differences between normal peer conflict and bullying.

Who Are the Bullies?

A common myth is that all bullies are boys. This is not true. Both girls and boys are bullies, but boys are more likely to admit to being one and are also easier to spot and identify because of the tactics they generally use.

The common stereotype of a bully as physically large, low achieving, and insecure is also not true. Bullies are not typically children who are failing academically. They are usually not the top students in a class, but they are likely to be average to just slightly below average in their achievement. Nor are they insecure and friendless. Bullies have friends, especially other children who empower them and are empowered by their association with the bully.

Recognizing the Difference

Normal Peer Conflict	Bullying
Equal power or friends	Imbalance of power; not friends
Happens occasionally	Repeated negative actions
Accidental	Purposeful
Not serious	Serious with threat of physical or emotional harm
Equal emotional reaction	Strong emotional reaction from victim and little or no emotional reaction from bully
Not seeking power or attention	Seeking power, control, or material things
Not trying to get something	Attempt to gain material things or power
Remorse — will take responsibility	No remorse — blames victim
Effort to solve the problem	No effort to solve problem

Table 1

Bullies are best identified by their **personality style** rather than by outward manifestations based on appearance, number of friends, or achievement:

▶ A bully is a child who values the rewards that aggression can bring.

▶ A bully is a child who lacks empathy for his or her victim and has difficulty feeling compassion.

▶ A bully tends to lack guilt. He or she fully believes that the victim provoked the attack and deserved the consequences.

▶ A bully likes to be in charge, to dominate, and to assert with power. A bully likes to win in all situations.

▶ A bully's parent(s) (or other significant role model) often model aggression.

▶ A bully thinks in unrealistic ways (e.g., "I should always get what I want.").

Depiction of Male Bullying
Drawn by a Sixth Grade Boy

Bullying Tactics

Boys tend to bully with aggressive tactics. Physical aggression is frequently used and it tends to be swift and effective. Tripping someone, a quick blow, or a knee in the stomach are all likely behaviors. Verbal aggression often accompanies the physical aggression or is used to threaten later physical consequences.

Girls tend to bully with social alienation and intimidation strategies (but not always—see *Figure 1*).

A victim might be teased about her clothing, gossiped about in a malicious manner, or become the recipient of intimidating notes. Some girls are targeted by cruel and demeaning extortion tactics with the promise of inclusion in a desired peer group if a specific act is performed. Female bullying is typically more insidious, cunning, and difficult to spot than is male bullying.

Depiction of Female Bullying
Drawn by a Sixth Grade Girl

A **passive victim** is likely to be a child who:

▶ Is isolated or alone during much of the school day.

▶ Is anxious, insecure, and lacking in social skills.

▶ Is physically weak and therefore unable to defend himself or herself.

▶ Cries easily, yields when bullied, and is unable to stick up for himself or herself.

▶ May have suffered past abuse or traumatization.

▶ May have a learning disorder that compromises his or her ability to process and respond to social interactional cues.

The New Kid on the Block
Jack Prelutsky

There's a new kid on the block,
and boy, that kid is tough,
that new kid punches hard,
that new kid plays real rough,
that new kid's big and strong,
with muscles everywhere,
that new kid tweaked my arm,
that new kid pulled my hair.

That new kid likes to fight,
and picks on all the guys,
that new kid scares me some,
(that new kid's twice my size),
that new kid stomped my toes,
that new kid swiped my ball,
that new kid's really bad,
I don't care for her at all.

—Prelutsky, 1984

Figure 1

The "Bullying Behaviors Chart" (see *Figure 2*) describes in more detail the specific tactics that bullies employ. These can range from mild name calling or shoving to very severe acts such as violence and coercion.

Who Are the Victims?

Children who are the victims of peer aggression and bullying are not randomly targeted as once believed, nor are they selected exclusively because of external appearance or disabilities. The victims of bullying are likely to be anxious, insecure children who lack social skills and the ability to defend themselves. They are often physically weak, cry easily, and are easy targets because they yield to bullying.

These children are referred to as **passive victims** or easy targets because they fail to fight back. Their "buttons" are easy to spot, making them targets for a bully.

There is another, smaller group of children who are likely to be victimized because of their provocative behavior. **Provocative victims** are children who are often restless, irritable, and who tease and provoke others. While these children will fight back to a point, they are ineffectual aggressors, and more frequently than not they end up losing the power struggle with the bullies and thus are also targets of bullying behavior.

This type of victim is more difficult to recognize than the passive victim, because he or she may be seen engaging the bully.

Bullying Behaviors Chart

	Mild		Moderate		Severe
Physical Agression:					
▶ Pushing ▶ Shoving ▶ Spitting	▶ Kicking ▶ Hitting	▶ Defacing property ▶ Stealing	▶ Physical acts that are demeaning and humiliating, but not bodily harmful (e.g., de-panting) ▶ Locking in a closed or confined space	▶ Physical violence against family or friends	▶ Threatening with a weapon ▶ Inflicting bodily harm
Social Alienation:					
▶ Gossiping ▶ Embarrassing	▶ Setting up to look foolish ▶ Spreading rumors about	▶ Ethnic slurs ▶ Setting up to take the blame	▶ Publicly humiliating (e.g., revealing personal information) ▶ Excluding from group ▶ Social rejection	▶ Maliciously excluding ▶ Manipulating social order to achieve rejection ▶ Malicious rumor-mongering	▶ Threatening with total isolation by peer group
Verbal Aggression:					
▶ Mocking ▶ Name calling ▶ Dirty looks ▶ Taunting	▶ Teasing about clothing or possessions	▶ Teasing about appearance	▶ Intimidating telephone calls	▶ Verbal threats of aggression against property or possessions	▶ Verbal threats of violence or of inflicting bodily harm
Intimidation:					
▶ Threatening to reveal personal information ▶ Graffiti ▶ Publicly challenging to do something	▶ Defacing property or clothing ▶ Playing a dirty trick	▶ Taking possessions (e.g., lunch, clothing, toys)	▶ Extortion ▶ Sexual/racial taunting	▶ Threats of using coercion against family or friends	▶ Coercion ▶ Threatening with a weapon

Copyright 1992 Garrity & Baris.

Figure 2

However, the provocative victim is really in over his or her head with the bully. Provocative victims are likely to exhibit the following characteristics:

▶ Are easily emotionally aroused.

▶ Tend to maintain the conflict and lose with frustration and distress.

▶ May be diagnosed with Attention Deficit Hyperactivity Disorder (ADHD).

▶ Have few or no friends (as distinguished from a bully who tends to have a cadre of followers who may appear to be friends).

Overall, these children are simply impulsive and action oriented. They may look like bullies at first glance but with a closer look it becomes obvious that two characteristics distinguish them. One is that they are not purposefully malicious and mean. Their actions are more impulsively driven than calculated. When they realize they have hurt another child, they will apologize after the fact and quickly resume what they were doing. These children are more oblivious than mean-spirited. Secondly, they typically lose when the bully turns on them. They are not as quick witted, mean-spirited, or cunning as the bully. The bully will overpower them and win.

Why, you may wonder, do bullies choose to pick on provocative victims? There appear to be a number of reasons. These children provoke the bully. They irritate others and the bully wants to show them who is boss. Picking on a provocative victim garners a lot of attention on the playground. Unlike the passive victims who cry and tremble, the provocative victims fight back with a great deal of gusto, noise, and bravado. This attracts attention. As one professional put it, "People's Court plays itself out right on the playground." Other children come running over to see what all the noise and commotion is about. Soon a crowd has gathered to watch. What could be more satisfying to a bully's need for power and domination than to have a large proportion of the school watch as he or she puts the victim in his or her place.

There is a third type of victim of bullying—the **vicarious victim.** This child is not the actual victim of bullying, but is acutely aware of the bullying that occurs. Vicarious victims have a moderate to high degree of sensitivity and empathy. Thus, they feel vulnerable to be a potential victim, and they feel sad for actual victims and guilty about their failure to help them.

The vicarious victim shares many of the characteristics and symptoms of other victims, particularly passive victims. They are often shy, anxious, and insecure. They lack confidence in their social skills and their ability to defend themselves or others. Their awareness of bullying make vicarious victims scared and withdrawn. They often develop physical symptoms like headaches, stomachaches and have trouble sleeping. Like other victims, they don't like school and may try to avoid going on a regular basis.

Bully-Victim Children

The two major subsets of children, bullies and victims, that have been previously described each have a unique set of descriptive characteristics. The descriptors for bullies are often the opposite of the descriptors for victims. For example, victims have low self-esteem and bullies have unrealistic self-esteem. Another example is bullies love power and victims are afraid. Yet there is a small group of children that seem to share the characteristics of both bullies and victims.

Theorists have sometimes thrown these children classified as bully-victims into the same group as provocative victims who are alternately labelled aggressive victims, ineffectual aggressors, and aggressive misfits. While both provocative victims and bully-victim children are described as being easily emotionally aroused and as emotionally reactive versus proactive aggressors (Stephenson and Smith, 1989), there are several things that differentiate the two groups. Provocative victims do not necessarily show aggression. They may be emotional and hyperactive (which is annoying to other children), but this differs from the aggression that characterizes bully-victim children. Some provocative victims do not report that they bully other children, while bully-victim children do report that they bully.

Olweus (1978) reports that about 10% of victims are provocative victims. Using the estimate that 20% of children are victims of school bullying, that would mean about 2% of children are provocative victims (Olweus, 1978). Olweus (1993) found that six percent of those who were seriously bullied, bullied others. Interestingly, Peplar, Craig, and Roberts (1998) did a survey in which 6% of the students reported themselves to be bullies, 15% reported being victims, and only 2% reported being both bullies and victims. But, Peplar, Craig, and Roberts' observational methods of documenting playground interaction showed that children switched between the role of bully and victim frequently.

Other research shows that this group of bully-victim children are more disturbed, depressed and anxious, and have poorer academic achievement than other children (Schwartz, 2000). Additionally, these children are more disliked in adolescent peer groups and are the ones for whom peers have the least empathy (Perry, Willard, and Perry, 1990). The FBI profiles of students who have done school shootings show that they have characteristics of both bullies and victims (Federal Bureau of Investigations, 2001). Clearly, this is a group with significant problems that needs attention in our bully-proofing intervention.

This group should be helped by bully-proofing intervention as they learn about the general problem of bullying and the issues involved for bullies and for victims. Although the caring majority students will begin standing up to them when they bully and protecting them when they are victimized, bully-victim children have a higher risk of serious aggression over time. It is recommended that the adults at a school be more vigilant with them and that some type of individualized intervention may also be necessary.

Bystanders

Bystanders are the third group of participants in bullying situations. They are the majority of students at a school (approximately 85% of the students) who watch bullying incidents and stand silently on the sideline not knowing what to do. They are also called the "silent majority." Because bullying usually happens when adults are not present or have their backs turned, the bystander children are a powerful resource for changing bullying dynamics at school. The aim of this program is to empower the bystanders so they can change from being a silent majority into a caring majority, eventually creating a caring community at their school.

Bystanders don't get involved in bullying events for a number of reasons. When asked why they don't try to help victims, bystander children say:

▶ They are scared the bully will turn on them or retaliate later.

▶ They don't know what to do.

▶ They are afraid they'll make things worse for the victim.

▶ They'll become less popular and be made fun of with the victim.

▶ They don't believe adults will really help.

These worries keep them immobilized. Yet this immobilization is harmful in the long run to bystanders. Over time bystander children are likely to become desensitized to bullying and its violence and cruelty and are likely to have a diminished capacity for empathy for the suffering of victims and people in general. The *Bully-Proofing* program, therefore, is especially important in maintaining the psychological well-being of bystanders.

Strategies for adults to use with bystander children include:

- normalizing their fears and worries

- emphasizing that there is strength in numbers

- reminding students that bully-proofing rules require them to take action

- reminding students of the CARES strategies for helping others

- acknowledging and rewarding caring behavior.

Conclusion

For all of these types of victims, the bully dominates and demonstrates power. This fuels the sense of power for the bully and he or she will come back again and again to prey on the same child. Sadly, a contagion effect can be put into motion on the school playground. Other children experience excitement and titillation watching the action play out. They watch, anxiously at first, and then seem to experience some vicarious thrill from the malicious behavior of one child against another. This sounds disturbing and hard to believe for many adults but it is not very different from the excitement adults derive from the violence in movies, on television, or on the nightly news. Bullying is exciting news on the childhood playground scene. Being part of the action may be both appealing and appalling at the same time. Some children make the decision to join with the bully both for the thrill of the ride and out of fear for their own well-being. A contagion grows. Soon the bully has far more children on his side and the victim is even more helpless and more at the mercy of the bully than ever. If this scene plays itself out day after day, the victim becomes miserable, desperate, and completely incapable of managing the situation. For these reasons, disciplinary action needs to be swift and "no-nonsense" in nature. This prevents the silent majority from joining the bully in the victimization.

The child who is the victim of a bully is probably suffering in silence. Children who are victimized usually don't tell and don't expect help. Many of them are highly vulnerable because of past abuse, loss, or learning disorders.

The consequences of sustained maltreatment over time has not been studied longitudinally, but it is likely that children who are the victims of bullying suffer from lowered self-esteem, fear and anxiety, disrupted academic performance, lack of interest in school, and a lack of trust and friends. Adults who were picked on by a bully during childhood can often recall the details of their traumatization with the same clarity as those who suffer from post-traumatic stress disorder. The effects of being the victim of a childhood bully may last a lifetime for some individuals.

Chapter Two

Intervention in Bullying Situations

The Need to Address the Problem

Children know who the bullies are and who the victims are long before the teachers and staff within a school do. Typically by six weeks into the school year the bully-victim interactional patterns have been established. Yet children do not tell on bullies. They don't tell because they are afraid. They are afraid that the bullying will become worse if they tell or that they might become the victim if they help someone else by telling. And sadly, most victims feel that no one will help them or be able to stop the bully even if they do tell.

Many bullies hide their bullying, especially with passive victims. It goes on "behind closed doors" so to speak, and there is a conspiracy of silence among the children. Most children are afraid to tell. They report that telling is ineffective and it only gets them into worse trouble. Research done in Canada confirms this (Craig & Pepler, 1995). When students report on bullying, most teachers and educators immediately confront the bully and demand an explanation of the behavior. Kids are smart. The bully knows who told and he or she will see to it that the student who ratted is certain not to do that again. The innocent bystanders watch and are thankful they were not involved. They, too, have learned the conspiracy of silence— don't tell or you will be next.

Another disturbing fact emerged from the Canadian research (Craig & Pepler, 1995). Cameras were hidden on the school playground and certain children wore hidden microphones. It was here that a bullying incident was recorded every seven minutes! In spite of teachers roaming the playground watching for bullying, almost all of it escaped detection by the eyes of the teachers yet the cameras caught it. Why? Because the children were clever. They knew not to bully in front of an adult. They didn't want to get caught. Bullying takes no longer than ten seconds to happen. A shove off the stairs, a quick punch, a threat, a put-down—any of these can be delivered so fast that an adult could not possibly see or hear the bullying from ten feet away.

This, indeed, was how most bullying was accomplished. It was done and over before anyone, other than the victim, even knew it had occurred. Sometimes it was disguised cleverly as playing, which the teachers failed to spot as an unfair game. For example, one girl was being guided about the playground with a jump rope tied around her neck. A group of girls were holding the rope as she walked in front of them. It appeared to be something the girl was acquiescing to and doing willingly. Later it was learned that the group of girls behind her were forcing her to go where they told her with threats of pulling the noose more tightly around her neck if she did not comply.

What is the lesson to be learned from these hidden cameras? They confirmed beyond a doubt that bullying goes on regularly and maliciously. They also confirmed that even the most alert and caring of teachers may not be able to spot it. It is a hidden phenomenon among children and the most efficient way to stop it is to teach the children who are there and aware of it to do something effective to intervene. Children can and will take action to protect the victim if they are part of a group and if they know they have the support of the school staff. A child must know that the bully will be widely identified, that something will be done, and that he or she will not be the only one who stood up for the victim. In other words, children must know that bullying will not be tolerated in their school.

Fears regarding telling are not figments of children's imaginations. Unfortunately, teachers often have difficulty distinguishing between true bullying and normal peer conflict. Thus, they may not realize the severity of a problem and fail to support the victim appropriately.

There is also a firmly held belief among classroom teachers and many parents that children benefit from learning to solve their own problems. Consequently, the most common response a child hears when he or she attempts to tell an adult is, "You are old enough now to solve your own problems." While this response rings true for normal peer conflict, victims of bullies are not old enough (or competent enough) to defend themselves.

Children cannot handle true bullying situations, and they do need help. Did you know? Dr. Dan Olweus (1991), who has researched bully-victim problems for over 20 years, found the **single most effective deterrent to bullying to be adult authority.** The adults in charge within a school need to learn to recognize bullying behavior and to stop it. Bully-proofing your school is essential if school is to be a safe and happy environment in which all the children can learn.

General Guidelines for Intervention

All children will be exposed to peer aggression at some point in their school experience. Most children can handle bullying that is in the mild to moderate range without adult assistance. **All children, however,** need help with bullying that is in the moderate to severe range.

One out of every seven children reports being involved in bullying experiences at school. Six percent are likely to be bullies while nine percent of children report being victims (Greenbaum, Turner, and Stephens, 1989). In an average elementary classroom of 20 children, there are most likely three children who need your help.

Help With Mild Bullying

In most cases, mild bullying behavior (refer back to *Figure 2*) can be overlooked by adults without detriment to the children involved. However, some children are not able to cope effectively with even mild bullying, and should be given adult assistance. These children include:

▶ Children who are shy or who lack social skills.

▶ Children who are isolated.

▶ Children who are learning disabled.

▶ Children who are repeatedly bullied.

▶ Children who have experienced a past trauma.

▶ Children who are using money or toys as bribes to protect themselves.

Help With Moderate to Severe Bullying

Adults should always intervene in moderate to severe bullying (refer back to *Figure 2*) situations. This is especially true if the **bullying has occurred more than once** and/or **the two children are not friends.** The "Developmental Guide to Conflict Resolution," shown in *Figure 3* provides a quick reference to intervention.

Developmental Guide to Conflict Resolution

The "Developmental Guide to Conflict Resolution" is a general reference to effective intervention tactics with children at various elementary ages involved in varying degrees of bullying. While this guide provides some helpful guidelines, the resolution suggestions are **not rules**—they are suggestions. The goals of conflict resolution as it is defined by this program are to:

▶ **become aware of your own predominant style** (e.g., "no-nonsense," "problem solver," "smoother," etc.)

▶ **respect it**

▶ **expand your repertoire** of conflict resolution approaches as much as possible

▶ **identify and rely upon staff members with styles that complement your own** (e.g., if a "smoothing" approach is necessary in a situation, and you happen to be a very straightforward "problem solver," call upon another staff member to intervene rather than addressing a situation in a manner that violates your predominant style).

Any of these conflict resolution styles may be appropriate with any age or type of conflict, depending upon the circumstances. However, one situation calls for a specific conflict resolution style—an incidence of **physically aggressive or violent behavior** (any situation in which anyone's physical safety is endangered). This type of situation **requires an immediate "no-nonsense" approach.**

Keep in mind that children at certain grade levels exhibit "typical" conflict behaviors, but some children are more or less mature than others of their age. As children mature, they become increasingly more capable of learning skills such as compromise and problem solving. Use your best judgment when examining a situation. Consider the maturity level of the children involved when selecting a conflict resolution tactic. Modeling these higher level

Depiction of Moderate/Severe Bullying
Drawn by a Fourth Grade Girl

Depiction of Moderate/Severe Bullying
Drawn by a Fourth Grade Boy

skills by your own interactions with both your peers and students will also promote and facilitate their adoption by the children around you.

Developmental Guide to Conflict Resolution

Grade Level	Typical Conflict	Preferred Styles of Resolution
1	Conflict likely over toys, possessions ("It's mine."), going first	▶ Action oriented ▶ Separate the children ▶ Change the topic ▶ **No-Nonsense** or **Smoothing**
1 and 2	Selfishness, wanting own way Threatening with tattling or not playing with again ("I'm not inviting you to my birthday.")	▶ Undo what the offender did ▶ **No-Nonsense** or **Problem Solving**
3, 4, and 5	What's fair and what isn't Teasing, gossiping, feeling superior Putting down, accusing of something not true or distorted	▶ Beginning stage of understanding others' intentions: mutual negotiation possible with help ▶ Compromise for older grade levels ▶ **Problem Solving** or **Compromising**
5 and 6	Bossiness, tattling, put-downs, showing off, betrayal	▶ Compromise can be used: empathy is possible at this age ▶ Talking things out, even if no compromise is reached ▶ **Ignoring** (only if a minor problem) or **Compromising**

Copyright 1991 by Binswanger-Friedman and Ciner.

Figure 3

Chapter Three
Student Instruction

The following lesson plans (seven Primary, K-1, and seven Intermediate, 2-6) are designed to be used in conjunction with the rest of the *Bully-Proofing Your School* program. It is important, at this point, to review the program philosophy before using the lesson plans. The **philosophy** of the classroom curriculum is based on the following principles:

‣ Adults must be involved in helping children deal with bullies because of the power imbalance that occurs in bullying situations.

‣ To stop bullying, we must shift the power from the bully or bullying group to the caring majority of students by: (1) setting explicit rules that say bullying is not allowed, and (2) by teaching all the students ways to speak out against bullying.

‣ It is important for the adults to convey a "can do" attitude. This means that the adults portray confidence in the belief that they can implement their program to prevent bullying and that the children can learn the techniques to prevent bullying.

‣ It is also important that the adults maintain a nonpunitive attitude. Bullies and victims should never be mentioned by name in the classroom group discussions, unless a student volunteers that information about himself or herself.

‣ Caring and compassion are valued attributes in children that must be verbally acknowledged and reinforced by the adults.

‣ Children learn social/emotional concepts best by discussion and modeling rather than by lecture. The more of the ideas that are generated by the children themselves, the better.

‣ Children learn social skills by trying them out themselves. This practice can best be accomplished by role play, puppet play, and storytelling by children.

SECTION ONE: Primary Curriculum (Grades K-1)

The seven week student instruction format has been used successfully with the first to fifth grade student population. When a school-wide bully-proofing program has been adopted, it is important to teach the common language of the program and introduce the protective strategies as early as possible. A modified curriculum has been developed to meet the unique needs of the kindergarten and first grade children (see Chapter One).

Providing children with an understanding of what bullying is and how to deal with it appropriately is the focus at this level. An emphasis is placed on understanding **friendship**. This starting point has proven to be an effective "jumping off" point to teach the language and strategies of bully-proofing.

Children can relate to the need for specific social skills instruction to effectively initiate and maintain friendships after understanding what a positive friendship looks and feels like. The protective strategies (Modified HA HA, SO) are taught and emerge as part of a discussion of what to do if kids are not being friendly. The difference between tattling and telling/reporting supports the CARES strategies—it is important to help **others** who are not being treated with kindness and respect. Teaching, modeling, and reinforcing children to perform random acts of kindness is a positive, proactive way to encourage moral development.

The primary curriculum (K–1) consists of six weekly lessons and a follow-up review lesson, which is conducted three to six weeks after the completion of this curriculum. The lessons can be led by the classroom teacher alone in his or her classroom, or ideally, with the assistance of the facilitator. **Each lesson typically lasts 20 to 30 minutes, but the curriculum is meant to be flexible. The age and attention span of younger students will vary. Lessons that appear to require more time can be extended or divided into multiple lessons, as the individual needs of the classes dictate.**

What I Want in a Friend

MATERIALS

Handout/Poster 1: "What I Want in a Good Friend" (or teacher alternate)

Book title: *Friends* by Helme Heine is recommended (or teacher alternate)

OBJECTIVES

To understand that friendship is positive in nature. To understand that friendship involves a number of characteristics.

STEPS

1. **Introduce the Concept of "Being a Friend"**
Teacher: "What do we look for in a friend?" Use examples such as: someone who listens when we talk, someone who cares about our feelings, someone who is kind to us.

   ▸ Teacher and/or facilitator can also give an example from a real-life friendship of his/her own.

   ▸ Introduce rules and expectations for classroom lessons for the group:

      1. Be respectful, no put-downs

      2. When sharing stories, do not mention any student names. Instead, say, "I know someone who ...."

2. **Explore Student's Ideas About "What Makes a Good Friend"**

   ▸ Brainstorm with the children, using an enlarged version of *Poster 1,* "What I Want in a Good Friend," to record children's ideas.

   ▸ Read a book that describes friendship. (*Friends* by Helme Heine is a good option.) Discuss the key points of the story, emphasizing the specific characteristics that help to make friendships positive. Stress the importance of caring about one another, being fair to each other, and having similar interests.

   ▸ Pass out the "What I Want in a Good Friend" handout (*Handout 1*) to each child. Students can either fill in the balloons with words or color in the balloons. Pictures can also be drawn on the back illustrating positive friendship skills.

3. **Review Concepts of Being a Good Friend**
Reinforce the following key points:

   ▸ Sharing

   ▸ Caring

   ▸ Being fair

   ▸ Having fun

   ▸ Having similar interests

   ▸ Celebrating differences

NEXT LESSON

In the next lesson, the students will discuss their current friendships as they continue to learn the skills necessary to initiate positive relationships.

RESOURCE GUIDE

See "Books for Primary Students" for ideas.

What I Want in a Good Friend

What I want
in a good friend

How to Make Friends

MATERIALS

Handout 2: Tips for Joining a Group of Kids

Book title: *How to Lose All Your Friends* by Nancy Carlson is recommended

Video title: *Hopscotch* (or teacher alternate)

OBJECTIVE

To develop the skills necessary to initiate friendships in a positive manner.

STEPS

1. **Last Lesson Review**
    Allow a few students to share their positive friendship experiences. Weave into the discussion a review of the characteristics necessary to help make friendships positive. Emphasize the importance that each and every person deserves to feel safe, have fun, and be treated kindly.

2. **Activities**
    Teacher: "Today we're going to talk about the do's and don'ts of making friends."

    ▶ Read a story or show a video that illustrates the do's and don'ts of making friends. (The video *Hopscotch* or book *How to Lose All Your Friends* by Nancy Carson are recommended.)

    ▶ Offer the children a chance to think and talk about what friendship means.

    ▶ Discuss why some people have trouble making friends.

▶ Teach 5 Good Tips for Joining a Group of Kids

1. Try to join with kids who are friendly.

2. Look for kids who enjoy the same activities you like.

3. Remember—it is easier to join one person or a group of four or more.

4. Remember—"no" does not mean "never."

5. Observe the activity you want to join first. Imitate, don't change what the other children are playing.

Practice the 5 tips with the children. To structure the role play, teacher and facilitator should participate.

▶ As an alternative, have the children role play appropriate ways to make friends, using puppets.

▶ Ask students to practice being a good friend at school, in the neighborhood, at soccer practice, etc. Request that they begin to notice who is being a good friend and report their observations during the next group session.

3. **Additional Activities**
    (These activities should be completed during one or more class sessions by the classroom teacher prior to the next lesson.)

    ▶ Encourage the students to talk about an experience in which they made a new friend. Was it hard? Easy? How did they feel? Ask students if they want to tell about an experience in which they tried but weren't able to

RESOURCE GUIDE

See "Videotapes and Films for Students" and "Books for Primary Students."

make a new friend. What went wrong? How could they have acted differently?

NEXT LESSON

In the next lesson, the children will learn the skills necessary to keep friends. The classroom rules and "no bullying" posters will be introduced.

Tips for Joining a Group of Kids

5 Good Tips for Joining a Group of Kids

1. Think about which kids are **friendly.** Try to join those kids.

2. Think about which kids like the **same things** you like. Try to join those kids.

3. It is easiest to join **one person** or a **group of four** or more.

4. Remember "**no**" does not always mean "never." It could mean "**not right now**" or "**try again later.**" So try at least three different times to join a group of kids (not always on the same day).

5. Observe the activity you want to join. Try to fit in by **imitating** what the others are doing. Do not try to change what the other children are playing.

How to Keep Friends

MATERIALS

Handout/Poster 10: Classroom Rules (or teacher alternate)

Handout/Poster 4: Modified Classroom Rules

Poster 11: The Bulldog (or teacher alternate)

Poster 12: "Don't Be a Bulldog!" (or teacher alternate)

Poster 13: "No Bullying Allowed!" (or teacher alternate)

Handout/Poster 3: Kids' Kindness Laws (or teacher alternate)

Books titles: *Bailey the Big Bully* by Lizi Boyd or *King of the Playground* by Phyllis Reynolds Naylor

Video title: *Standing Up for Yourself* (or teacher alternate)

OBJECTIVE

To develop the skills necessary to maintain friendships.

STEPS

1. **Last Lesson Review**
   Ask the students to recall and/or demonstrate the steps needed to initiate positive friendships. Ask students, "Who did you notice being a good friend this week?" Teachers and facilitators may share their observations also.

2. **Activities**
   Teacher: "Today we are going to talk about what kind of behavior is called bullying." You may want to set a ground rule, for discussions whereby a student's name may only be used if something positive is shared.

▶ Choose a book or video that is an appropriate level and describes bullying behavior, as defined in the basic curriculum. The book, *Bailey the Big Bully* by Lizi Boyd is highly recommended. An alternate book choice is Phyllis Reynolds Naylor's *King of the Playground.* The video *Standing Up for Yourself* is a good alternative to reinforce and illustrate the concept of bullying versus normal peer conflict. Ask the children to first share their definition of "Bullying." It is important to understand the difference between normal peer conflict and bully behavior at a developmental level they can comprehend.

A Point to Emphasize
Friends have times when they do not get along well, but this is **not** bullying. Bullying usually does not occur between friends. Letting students know that if they feel like they don't have as much power as another child and/or they don't feel "safe" (both with their feelings and bodies), it might be a bully situation.

▶ Discuss the difference between friends not getting along well/normal peer conflict versus bullying. The teacher and/or facilitator can give a few examples for students to evaluate.

Example 1
Normal Peer Conflict
A classmate takes a book you want to read. You say you want it. The classmate says "no" and walks away.

Bullying
For the third time this week, a classmate

RESOURCE GUIDE

See "Books for Primary Students" or "Video-tapes and Films for Students," which feature the issue of bullying.

takes the book you want to read off your desk and gestures in a threatening way so no one can see him/her. You are feeling unsafe in your own classroom.

Example 2
Normal Peer Conflict
You're in line, waiting for the swing, when someone cuts in front of you, causing you to miss your turn.

Bullying
You are standing alone outside of school, waiting for the bell to ring. A group of older students begin to make fun of what you are wearing. They have gotten you upset before and seem determined to do the same thing again.

3. **Introduce the Classroom Rules and the "No Bullying" Posters**
Present the following classroom rules or your alternate rules about bullying:

   1. We will not bully other students.

   2. We will help others who are being bullied by speaking out and by getting adult help.

   3. We will use extra effort to include **all students** in activities at our school.

   You may want to reword rule #3 as "You can't say, 'you can't play'" (Paley, 1992) and the goal as "we all have the right not to have our bodies or our feelings hurt." Mount the rules on construction paper and tell the students you are going to hang the rules and some posters around the classroom to remind them of how bullying is no longer allowed!

   Teacher Tip
   "The Modified Classroom Rules" (*Handout/Poster 4*) may be more appropriate for classes where students are young developmentally.

   Alternate Activity
   Instead of or in addition to hanging up Posters 5 and 6 provided with this program, you may wish to have the students draw or color their own posters about bullying. You could then hang

their posters on a special "no-bullying" display.

4. **Additional Activity**
(This should be completed during one class session by the classroom teacher prior to the next lesson.)

   Kids' Kindness Laws
   After the classroom rules are developed, those students who are capable of writing can fill out *Handout/Poster 3*: "Kids' Kindness Laws." This would be an excellent activity to stress the importance of treating others with kindness as a critical step to developing and maintaining positive friendships.

NEXT LESSON

In the next lesson, the students will learn strategies that they can use when they are being victimized by a bully.

Kids' Kindness Laws

Kids' Kindness Laws

Write 5 "Kids' Kindness Laws" that would make this class a happier place for everyone.

1. _____

2. _____

3. _____

4. _____

5. _____

Write 2 things you already do to be kind.

1. _____

2. _____

Write 1 thing you might do today to be kind.
Pick something you don't do a lot.

_____

_____

_____

Reprinted with permission from Huggins, P. (1993). *Teaching friendship skills: Primary version.* Longmont, CO: Sopris West.

Modified Classroom Rules

Rules For a Bully-Free Classroom

1. No Bullying

2. Help Each Other

3. Include Everyone

What to Do if Kids Are Not Being Friendly

MATERIALS

Handout/Poster 5: Modified HA HA, SO Strategies

Handout 6: Modified HA HA, SO Shield

Book titles: *Move Over, Twerp* by Martha Alexander or *Chrysanthemum* by Kevin Henkes

Video title: *Standing Up for Yourself* (or teacher alternate)

OBJECTIVE

To teach the students strategies that they can use when they are being victimized by a bully.

STEPS

1. **Last Lesson Review**
   Ask the students to recall the classroom rules. Provide time on a daily basis to applaud friendly behavior and problem-solve issues as they arise. This discussion works well after recess time. Input from the playground supervisor, where appropriate, can be helpful.

2. **Ways to Handle Bullying**
   Teacher: "Today we will be talking about ways to handle bullying."

   ▶ To refamiliarize the students with friendly behavior vs. bullying situations and break the ice, read a story or show a video that is suitable to the age group of the children and **emphasizes appropriate responses** to being bullied. The books *Move Over, Twerp* by Martha Alexander or *Chrysanthemum* by Kevin Henkes are highly recommended. The video *Standing Up for Yourself* is another good choice.

   ▶ Teach and Model for the Students the Modified HA HA, SO Strategies

   Modified Protective Strategies may be more appropriate when working with young children. The language and complexity level is more easily understood.

   • Get Help: Go for help—it's not "tattling" when you feel unsafe.

   • Stand Up for Yourself: Be strong, you are important.

   • Walk Away: Stay away or find another way.

   • Say Good Things to Yourself: Think!! Build yourself up—NOT down.

   Teacher Tips for the Modified HA HA, SO Strategies
   Illustrate the following student strategies by using examples that occur frequently in your classroom:

   1. Get Help: Be sure to get help if you feel your safety is threatened in any way. This includes threats to your body and your feelings.

   2. Stand Up for Yourself: Use "I" statements. "I feel hurt when you say that" or "I don't like it when you talk to me that way" are examples.

   3. Walk Away: Leave the situation immediately. Don't respond with

RESOURCE GUIDE

See "Videotapes and Films for Students" and "Books for Primary Students" for materials suggestions.

words. **Get away** or stay away to begin with. Remember, there is safety in numbers. Play with children on the playground and walk home with other children if it helps you avoid being bullied.

4. Say Good Things to Yourself: Use affirmations such as, "I'm a nice person. I deserve to be treated kindly." This strategy can be paired with other strategies. This can be good follow-up to get you through a conflict or a tough situation.

HA HA, SO Shield Activity
Use *Handout 6* to illustrate how and when to use what strategy. Use concrete examples relevant to your student's experiences. It is also important to emphasize that what works for one student may not be appropriate or may not work for another. There is no one right way to handle a bullying situation **unless** you feel unsafe, which means you always need to **get help**.

NEXT LESSON

In the next lesson, students will learn the difference between "Tattling and Telling" and will begin to review skills they have been taught to this point.

Modified HA HA, SO Strategies

Bully-Proofing

1. GET HELP

2. STAND UP FOR YOURSELF

3. WALK AWAY

4. SAY GOOD THINGS TO YOURSELF

Modified HA HA, SO Shield

Get Help

Stand Up for Yourself

**Say Good Things
to Yourself**

Walk Away

Friends Get Help for Friends

MATERIALS

Handout/Poster 14: The Difference Between Tattling and Telling

Book title: *Tattlin' Madeline* by Carol Cummings is recommended (or teacher alternate)

OBJECTIVE

To understand the difference between "tattling" and "telling."

STEPS

1. **Last Lesson Review**
    Check that students still remember protective strategies.

2. **Activities**
    Teacher: "Today we are going to talk about the difference between 'tattling' and 'telling'."

    To clarify the difference between "telling" and "tattling," read a story or show a video that addresses this issue. (The book *Tattlin' Madeline* by Carol Cummings is strongly recommended for this purpose.) Ask the children to be "Detectives" to see how many protective strategies (HA HA, SO) they can pick out from the story or video. After the story or video, lead a class discussion that promotes an understanding of the differences between "telling/reporting" and "tattling." If something **dangerous, unsafe, or important** happens then it is important to "**tell**" an adult. If something **harmless, unimportant, or irritating** happens and the child does not feel "unsafe" or "powerless"—then it might be considered "tattling" if he or she reports it to an adult.

Using *Handout/Poster 14* have students practice understanding when it's "tattling" and when it is "telling." Expand upon the following examples to include situations that occur in the classroom or on the playground.

Examples of "Tattling"

▶ Someone cuts in front of you in line, but doesn't hurt you in the process.

▶ The teacher asks all students to complete a color, cut, paste activity. You notice a student at your table is playing with a puzzle.

Examples of "Telling"

▶ You see children fighting on the playground.

▶ A student or adult threatens to hurt you.

▶ Even after you try to walk away or stand up for yourself, a child keeps calling you very cruel names.

3. **Additional Activity**
    (This activity is ongoing and not limited to teaching prior to the next lesson.)

    Make a chart and post it in the classroom for ongoing input from students. Have the two categories be "tattling" and "telling." With teacher guidance, students can illustrate examples by drawing or writing (depending on ability) and post them under the correct category. This can be a useful tool for class discussions. The more **visual** and **concrete**, the better.

Teacher Tip
This lesson is sometimes presented after Lesson 1 due to the severity of "tattling" in some classrooms.

RESOURCE GUIDE

See "Books for Primary Students."

It is important for children to feel like they can come to you. Tattling behavior is sometimes the only way a child knows to get **attention**. A response to this behavior by the teacher can be "I'm glad you know the rule, " as you guide them in understanding the differences between "tattling" and "telling." In addition, provide the attention they may be seeking and look into possible social skills problems that may be interfering with friendships.

NEXT LESSON

In the next lesson, the children will be introduced to the "I Caught You Caring" program. You may need badges duplicated and may want to bring candy or stickers to be used to teach the concept of a "Random Act of Kindness."

Friends and Caring Acts of Kindness

MATERIALS

Handout/Poster 7: "Caught Caring" Slips

Handout 33: CARES Buttons

Candy, Stickers, or Teacher's Choice (optional)

Book title: *Kids' Random Acts of Kindness* by the editors of Conari Press

OBJECTIVE

To teach students that each one of them can make a difference. As a group they make up the "Caring Community" where kind and caring acts will be acknowledged and encouraged.

STEPS

1. **Last Lesson Review**
   Check that the students still remember the difference between "tattling" and "telling."

2. **Activities**
   Teacher: "Today we will be talking about "random acts of kindness," simply doing nice things for each other "just because." Hand out candy, stickers, or teacher's choice. When everyone has received a piece of candy, for example, explain that you wanted to do something nice for each of them "just because." Ask the students how they like this surprise. Explain that it feels good to have given them a treat. In other words, it was a "win-win" situation because both parties felt good

about the candy surprise. This describes what a Random Act of Kindness is like.

Note: You can also substitute five minutes of free time for candy to illustrate a Random Act of Kindness.

Read a few excerpts from *Kids' Random Acts of Kindness* by the editors of Conari Press or a teacher alternate. After a few examples, the children should be able to share their own experiences of giving and receiving random acts of kindness.

Introduce the "I Caught You Caring" Reinforcement Program
These daily or weekly sessions are designed for reinforcement of caring behavior within the classroom. They can occur at the end of the week for older students, and take five to ten minutes. Younger students may require more frequent recognition, even daily. Each teacher chooses one or more of his or her students, who he or she "caught" being kind or helpful to another student for this special recognition. The teacher should keep a log of "acts of kindness" that he or she notices during the day or week, and then pick a good example—or more—to reinforce.

3. **Additional Activities**
   (These ideas are suggested as "ongoing activities" to help keep the momentum going to encourage a kind and caring climate in the classroom.)

"I Caught You Caring" Alternative Program Ideas

▶ "Caught Caring" slips can be filled out and displayed on class bulletin boards. (See *Handouts 33* and *7*.)

RESOURCE GUIDE

See "Books for Primary Students."

- Budding artists and writers love to "publish" their own books. A sample title: "Random Acts of Kindness in (Teacher's Name)'s Room."

- Students can design their own badges. The nomination process works the same way as "I Caught You Caring" program. Teachers can display the badges. Typically badges are worn for one day; students then return them to the teacher.

Teacher's Tip
Remember to stress to children the importance of helping children who are being bullied. Remind them that "kindness is contagious." The teacher should keep things going daily. The classroom "climate" should reflect a safe, positive, inclusive, friendly environment where every individual **deserves** to be treated with respect and kindness. Uncaring, bully behavior will not be tolerated.

NEXT LESSON

The next lesson is a follow-up session to be conducted in about three to six weeks. During the follow-up review lesson, the facilitator will: (1) evaluate student progress and determine whether any new problems have surfaced, (2) review and reinforce the student skills to prevent bullying and reinforce positive friendship-making skills, and (3) provide any additional instruction necessary to ensure the continued success of the program.

Caught Caring

CAUGHT CARING

Name _____

How _____

_____

_____

Signature _____

CAUGHT CARING

Name _____

How _____

_____

_____

Signature _____

CAUGHT CARING

Name _____

How _____

_____

_____

Signature _____

CAUGHT CARING

Name _____

How _____

_____

_____

Signature _____

Review Lesson

MATERIALS

Refer back to any handouts/posters from Lessons 1–6 relating to skills to reinforce and review, including:

Poster/Handout 2: Tips for Joining a Group of Kids

Handout/Poster 5: Modified HA HA, SO Strategies

Handout 33: CARES Buttons

Handout 6: Modified HA HA, SO Shield

Handout/Poster 14: The Difference Between Tattling and Telling

OBJECTIVES

To revisit the classroom three to six weeks after the classroom curriculum was taught to: (1) evaluate student progress and determine whether any new problems have surfaced, (2) review and reinforce the student skills to prevent bullying behavior and reinforce positive friendship-making skills, and (3) provide any additional instruction necessary to ensure the continued success of the program.

Evaluate Student Progress

Before the review lesson, discuss with the classroom teacher his or her perceptions of student progress. Find out whether any new problems have surfaced in the classroom and/or observations of positive changes.

Reteach Any Skills Specifically Related to Any Problems Identified in the Class Discussion

Based on the feedback from the classroom teacher, reteach all or applicable parts of the lessons addressing deficient skills. During the lesson with the students, review and discuss problems and applaud successes in that specific classroom.

Conclude the Lesson

Summarize for the students that they have learned these important things about friendship: (1) what it is, (2) how to make and keep friends, (3) what they can do if a bully picks on them, (4) what to do if they see a bully picking on someone else, and (5) how kind and caring acts can become contagious. Remind them that they will have to keep practicing these strategies to get good at them and that their teacher will be available to help them if they have any questions or need help practicing.

SECTION TWO:
Intermediate Curriculum (Grades 2-6)

The intermediate curriculum is designed for students in grades 2 through 6. It consists of six weekly lessons and a follow-up review lesson, which is conducted three to six weeks after the completion of this curriculum. The lessons can be led by the classroom teacher alone or with the assistance of a facilitator. **Each lesson typically lasts 30 to 45 minutes.**

The Concept of Bullying

MATERIALS

The Colorado School Climate Student Report (optional, available in the *Bully-Proofing Your School: Administrator's Guide to Staff Development*)

Handout 8: Recognizing the Difference

Handout 9: Optional Sociogram

OBJECTIVES

To introduce the concept of bullying to the students (including information about bullying tactics and the types of children likely to be bullies and victims) to determine the extent of bullying occurring in the classroom.

STEPS

1. **Introduce the Concept of Bullying to the Students**
   Teacher: "Today we are going to be discussing the topic of bullying. We'll be talking about what bullying is, why some kids bully and how they bully, and the characteristics of the kids who are bullies and of the kids who are victims. We'll discuss how bullying is different from normal peer conflict that happens between friends and why bullying is harmful for the victims and for the bullies. When we are talking about bullying, you may think of examples from here at school or in your neighborhood. I'll want to hear these examples, but I'll ask you not to use specific names. Instead, say 'someone I know' or 'a girl in our neighborhood.' Well, let's get started. Does anyone have some ideas on what bullying is?"

Write students' ideas on the board. Then make sure the students have included the following items by adding them to the list on the board:

▶ An imbalance of power (psychological, physical, or social);

▶ Repeated incidences of negative actions, not just one time (unless very severe);

▶ Done by either a single individual or a group;

▶ Done to gain attention or popularity;

▶ Done to get one's way or material things; and

▶ Between children who are not friends and don't usually play together.

2. **Discuss Why Children Bully Others**
   Teacher: "Now let's discuss why children bully others. Who has an idea on why kids bully."

Again write the students' ideas on the board and then make sure that the following ideas are included in their list by adding them:

▶ to get power,

▶ to gain popularity and attention or material things,

▶ to act out problems at home,

▶ to copy what another person they may admire does,

▶ to have fun, and

▶ to act out unresolved emotional issues.

3. **Discuss What Types of Children Are Likely to Be Bullies**
Teacher: "What types of children are likely to be bullies? Any other ideas?"

Again write the students' ideas on the board and then make sure that the following ideas are included in their list by adding them:

▶ A child who likes the rewards that aggression can bring.

▶ A child who lacks compassion for his or her victim.

▶ A child who lacks guilt.

▶ A child who believes that the victim provoked his or her attack and deserved what happened.

▶ A child who likes to be in charge and to get his or her own way with power.

▶ A child whose parent(s) (or older brothers and sisters) are bullying him or her.

▶ A child who misperceives how others treat him or her.

4. **Discuss How Children Bully**
Teacher: "How do children bully other children? What kinds of things do they do?"

List students' ideas on the board. Then teach the students the four general categories of bullying behavior:

▶ By physical aggression (e.g., spitting, tripping, pushing, shoving, destroying another's things, hitting, threatening with a weapon);

▶ By social alienation (e.g., gossiping, spreading rumors, ethnic or racial slurs, excluding from a group, publicly humiliating, threatening with total isolation from the peer group);

▶ By verbal aggression (e.g., mocking, name calling, teasing, intimidating telephone calls, verbal threats of aggression); and

▶ By intimidation (e.g., graffiti, a public challenge to do something, playing a dirty trick, taking possessions, coercion).

Now go back through the list on the board and have the students help categorize the behaviors by writing a "P" for "physical," "S" for "social," "V" for "verbal," and "I" for "intimidation" next to it.

5. **Discuss What Types of Children Are Likely to Be Victims**
Teacher: "Now let's discuss what types of children are likely to be the victims of bullies. Who has an idea on this topic?"

Again write the students' ideas on the board and then make sure that the following ideas are included in their list by adding them:

▶ A child who is isolated and alone during much of the school day.

▶ A child who is anxious, insecure, and has trouble making friends.

▶ A child who is small or weak and therefore unable to defend himself or herself.

▶ A child who cries easily, gives up when bullied, and is unable to successfully stick up for himself or herself.

▶ A child who may have suffered past abuse at home.

▶ A child who may have a learning disability.

▶ A child who is willing to keep quiet.

Sometimes a victim (even though he or she may not seem like a victim) is:

▶ A child who is often restless, irritable, and who teases and provokes other children.

▶ A child who will fight back, but ends up losing.

▶ A child who tries not to give in to the bully, and gets very upset when he or she does lose.

6. **Discuss the Difference Between Normal Peer Conflict and Bullying**
Teacher: "It helps us understand what bullying is to compare it to normal peer conflict that might come up with your friends. This chart (use *Handout 8*) shows some of the differences."

Bullying is different from regular conflict because it involves danger—the danger of someone being physically and/or emotionally hurt. For example, if a child teasingly sits in another's chair, there really is not any danger. This is a normal peer conflict. But if a child is repeatedly called names, this can result in harm to that child's self-esteem, so it is dangerous.

7. **Discuss the Emotional Consequences for the Victim**
Teacher: "Bullying is dangerous to the victim. What are some of the bad effects that can happen to the person who is bullied?"

Again list student ideas and make sure the following are included:

▶ Drop in self-esteem to self-defeating, fearful attitude;

▶ Feeling scared, withdrawn, isolated, and/or sad;

▶ Physical symptoms (e.g., headache, stomachache, general fatigue);

▶ Not liking school; and

▶ Panic and irrational retaliation.

8. **"The Colorado School Climate Student Report" (optional)**
If you would like to get a copy of the "Colorado School Climate Student Report" please see *Bully-Proofing Your School: Administrator's Guide to Staff Development.*

9. **Scoring the "Optional Sociogram"**
Questions A, B, and C from "The Social Survey" (*Handout 9*) may be used for a sociogram at each elementary grade level. Begin with a list of all the students at a grade level within your school or in one specific classroom at a grade level. Put a plus sign (+) next to a child's name each time he or she is listed in response to Question A. Put a minus sign (-) next to a child's name each time he or she is listed in response to Question B. Put a zero (0) next to a child's name each time he or she is listed in responses to Question C. Popular children will end up with many plus signs, bullies with a mixture of plus and minus signs, provocative victims with many minus signs and zeros, and passive victims will end up with many zeros.

The sociogram helps teachers assess social interactional patterns within a grade level or classroom. It is an easy way to identify the socially isolated students.

NEXT LESSON

In the next lesson, the students will be given the classroom rules and "no-bullying" posters will be introduced. (If you obtained the "Colorado School Climate Student Report," feedback can also be given to students in the next lesson.)

Recognizing the Difference

Normal Peer Conflict	Bullying
Equal power or friends	Imbalance of power; not friends
Happens occasionally	Repeated negative actions
Accidental	Purposeful
Not serious	Serious with threat of physical or emotional harm
Equal emotional reaction	Strong emotional reaction from victim and little or no emotional reaction from bully
Not seeking power or attention	Seeking power, control, or material things
Not trying to get something	Attempt to gain material things or power
Remorse — will take responsibility	No remorse — blames victim
Effort to solve the problem	No effort to solve problem

Optional Sociogram

Social Survey

A. List the three children in your grade who you most like to do things with:

_____

_____

_____

B. List the three children in your grade who you don't like to spend time with:

_____

_____

_____

C. List the three children in your grade who you think most need a friend:

_____

_____

_____

Rules for Bully-Proofing the Classroom

MATERIALS

Handout/Poster 10: Classroom Rules (or teacher alternate)

Poster 11: The Bullydog

Poster 12: "Don't Be a Bullydog!" (or teacher alternate)

Poster 13: "No Bullying Allowed!" (or teacher alternate)

Handout/Poster 14: The Difference Between Tattling and Telling

OBJECTIVES

To introduce some key concepts (e.g., the difference between tattling and getting adult help), to present the classroom rules about bullying that the students will be expected to abide by, and to provide feedback about student responses to "The Colorado School Climate Student Report" if it was done.

STEPS

1. **Last Lesson Review**
   Ask the students to recall the definition of bullying, why someone might bully, and who is likely to be a victim.

2. **Present the Goal of This Program**
   Assure the students that you and they together are going to make the classroom **safe** for all people from now on. Let them know that **no physical or verbal bullying will be allowed.**

3. **Present Key Program Concepts**

   ▶ Introduce the idea of bully-proofing.

   The adults in your school have been trained and will help to keep you safe.

   ▶ Introduce the concept that strength is found in numbers.

   If a bully is trying to be popular, then having most of the class saying, "I don't like what you are doing" will stop the bully from achieving that goal. It is difficult for the bully to target a victim if children stick together and no one is left out.

   ▶ Explain the difference between tattling and getting adult help (use *Handout/Poster 14* here if needed).

   It is not tattling when you help someone who is in danger, who is being hurt physically or emotionally, by speaking out. The goal of telling an adult is to get help, not to get someone in trouble.

   It might be helpful to model speaking out about bullying for the students, and to give the students some examples to cement their understanding of the difference between "tattling" and "getting adult help." Two examples to discuss are: "Jimmy took my place in line. Teacher, make him move," and "Susie is calling me 'Four Eyes' again. Teacher, I need help." Have the students vote on whether each example is tattling or getting adult help.

4. **Introduce the Classroom Rules**
   Present the following classroom rules about bullying or your own:

   1. We will not bully other students.

   2. We will help others who are being bullied by speaking out and by getting adult help.

   3. We will use extra effort to include **all students** in activities at our school.

   Explain to the students that the goal is for everyone to be physically and emotionally safe. For primary students, you may want to reword rule #3 as "You can't say, 'You can't play' " (Paley, 1992) and the goal as "We all have the right to have our bodies or our feelings be safe."

5. **Introduce the "No-Bullying" Posters**
   Present the students with *Handout/Poster 10, Poster 11, Poster 12* and *Poster 13*. Tell the students that you are going to hang these posters, along with the classroom rules around the room to remind them that bullying is no longer allowed in their classroom.

6. **Feedback (optional)**
   Give the students feedback about their class' responses to "The Colorado School Climate Student Report" (if you obtained the results).

   For primary students (grades 1, 2, and 3): Feedback may be general rather than specific. For example:

   "Bullying is a problem in this classroom."

For intermediate students (grades 4, 5, and 6): More specific feedback about problem areas may be given. For example:

"In your class, there is a problem with teasing (or getting hurt physically)."

"More girls than boys in your class reported being bullied."

"Many children in your class need a friend."

Facilitator Notes

Remember to never identify by name or insinuation who the bullies are or who the victims are during any of the class discussions. This could embarrass the students, and thus cause resistance to the program.

Alternate Activity

Instead of or in addition to hanging up *Posters 12* and *13* provided with this program, you may wish to have the students draw or color their own posters about bullying (both male and female). You could then hang all their posters on a special no-bullying display, or even have a poster contest.

NEXT LESSON

In the next lesson, the students will learn strategies that they can use when they are being victimized by a bully.

Classroom Rules

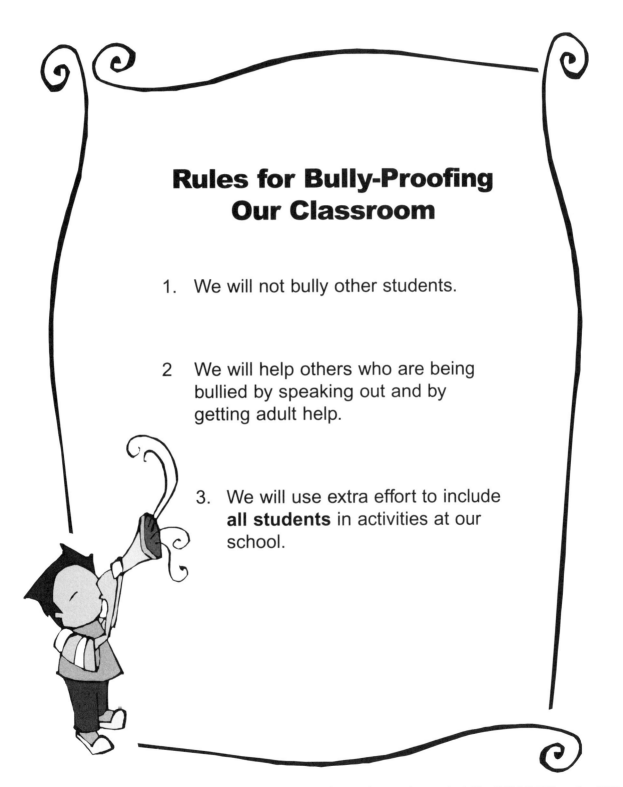

Rules for Bully-Proofing Our Classroom

1. We will not bully other students.

2 We will help others who are being bullied by speaking out and by getting adult help.

3. We will use extra effort to include **all students** in activities at our school.

The Bullydog

"Don't Be a Bullydog!"

Don't Be a

Bullydog!

"No Bullying Allowed!"

Teaching Strategies for the Victims

MATERIALS

Handout/Poster 14: The Difference Between Tattling and Telling

Poster 15: HA HA, SO

Handout 16: Skills to Disengage

Handout 17: "Pushing Your Buttons"

Handout 18: HA HA, SO Shield

OBJECTIVES

To teach the students strategies that they can use when they are being victimized by a bully—"HA HA, SO."

STEPS

1. **Last Lesson Review**
   Ask the students to recall the classroom rules.

2. **Group Activity**
   To refamiliarize the students with bullying situations and break the ice, read a story from your school's library or show a video that addresses a bully-victim situation. Be sure to select one that is appropriate to the age group of the children.

3. **Teach and Model for the Students the HA HA, SO Strategies**

   HA HA, SO

H - Help	H - Humor	S - Self-Talk
A - Assert Yourself	A - Avoid	O - Own It

   ▶ **Help**—Teach the students when and how to seek help from peers and/or an adult.

This strategy is best used in situations where help is available and willing, like at a "bully-proofed school." A victim can use this strategy during a bullying situation by calling to some other children, for example, "Could you help me ask Teddy to stop taking my books away from me?" or by running to an adult, describing what is happening, and saying, "I need help." Refer to *Handout/Poster 14*, "Tattling or Telling," and have students brainstorm and discuss the differences between these behaviors.

A victim can also use this strategy when anticipating a bullying situation by asking several other children to stay close. For example, "Susan and her friends have been bullying me at recess. Could you play with me today and help me figure out what to do if they come at me again?" or by informing the teacher and asking for a watchful eye. It can be helpful to have each student think of and name at least one adult and one peer he or she can turn to for help.

▶ **Assert Yourself**—Teach the students when it would be wise to use assertiveness and when it would not.

This strategy is usually the best strategy for a victim to start with. But it should not be used with severe bullying or when the victim is very scared. To use this strategy, the victim looks the bully in the eye and says, for example, "I don't like how you are gossiping about me and trying to make me have no friends. It is mean and unfair. Stop doing it."

RESOURCE GUIDE

See "Videotapes and Films for Students," "Books for Primary Students," or "Books for Intermediate Students" for materials that address bullying situations.

RESOURCE GUIDE

See "Books for Primary
Students" or "Books for
Intermediate Students"
for books that feature
the use of humor in bul-
lying situations.

▶ **Humor**—Teach the students how to use humor to de-escalate a situation.

This strategy is fun for children and can be used in conjunction with the "Help" strategy by asking other children to help dream up humorous ways to deal with a certain bullying situation. Several of the books listed in the Resource Guide illustrate humor as a strategy for dealing with the bully (e.g., in *Loudmouth George and the Sixth Grade Bully*, the victim, with the help of his friend, makes a horrific lunch with pickles in the sandwich and hot chili sauce in the thermos for a bully who has been stealing his lunch). The victim could also use this strategy by writing a funny note or poem to the bully.

▶ **Avoid**—Teach the students how to walk away in order to avoid a bullying situation.

This strategy may be best for situations when the victim is alone. One way for the victim to use the "Avoid" strategy is to avoid a bully physically. The victim can cross the street or can avoid the situation(s) where the bullying is occurring. The victim can also avoid a bully by being with others rather than alone, perhaps by asking to walk home from school with other children. Another way for the victim to use the "Avoid" strategy is to analyze the situation and to stop doing anything that might be provoking the bully. If the bullying is happening when the class lines up and both the victim and the bully want to be at the front of the line, the victim can choose to be at the end of the line in order to avoid a bullying situation.

▶ **Self-Talk**—Teach the students how to use their self-talk to maintain positive self-esteem during a bullying situation.

Remind the students that in Session 1 they learned how victims' self-esteem drops when they are being bullied. The "Self-Talk" strategy is used to keep feeling good about oneself. The strategy involves "putting on a record in one's mind" that says nice things like: "I'm a good kid. I try my best at school and I'm nice to other kids. When Jason calls me dumb, it is not my fault. It is his problem that he is being mean. It is unfair. I don't have to accept his opinion of me. I can have my own opinion about me and I like myself."

▶ **Own It**—Teach the students how to "own" the put-down or belittling comment in order to defuse it.

This strategy can be combined with the "Humor" strategy with responses like, "I agree that this is an ugly dress; my mother made me wear it." It can also be combined with the "Assert Yourself" strategy with responses like, "I do have slanted eyes and that is because I'm Korean. Korea is a really cool country. Do you want to hear some things about it?"

Explain to the students that the first strategy that they try with a bully may not work. In that case, they will have to try another. That is why you are giving them six strategies and an easy way to remember them (HA HA, SO)—so that they will have lots of things to try. After they know the six strategies really well, they will be able to quickly figure out which strategy to try first, second, and so on, in each unique bullying situation.

As an indication of their understanding of these strategies, ask the class to identify the strategy or strategies used by the victim character in the story or video you presented to the class at the beginning of this session. If none of the HA HA, SO strategies were used, ask the students to identify a strategy or strategy that the victim character **should have** used.

To reinforce the memorization of the HA HA, SO mnemonic, you may wish to have the students repeat the strategies in some way, such as singing HA HA, SO to a familiar tune, calling out the strategies as you yell the HA HA, SO "cheer" (i.e., "Give me an H!" "Help!" "Give me an A!" "Assert Yourself!" and so on), or by any other means you can think of that would be fun and memorable for the students.

Hang *Poster 15* up in the classroom with the other bullying posters to remind the students about the strategies they can use when they are being bullied.

4. **Having Students Think About how to use HA HA, SO Strategies**
Handouts 16, 17, and *18* can be used to teach students how to disengage from a bully's attempts to push their buttons and how to use HA HA, SO as a protective shield to cover their buttons.

NEXT LESSON

In the next lesson, the students will have the opportunity to try these strategies themselves, and practice them to a comfort level through role play.

The Difference Between Tattling and Telling

Tattling	vs.	Telling
Unimportant		Important
Harmless		Harmful or dangerous physically or psychologically
Can handle by self		Need help from an adult to solve
Purpose is to get someone in trouble		Purpose is to keep people safe
Behavior is accidental		Behavior is purposeful

HA HA, SO

What I Can Do if I Am Being Bullied

HA	HA	SO
Help	**H**umor	**S**elf-Talk
Assert Yourself	**A**void	**O**wn It

Skills to Disengage

1. Think about what gets to you.

   What are your buttons?

2. When you find someone has pushed one of your buttons, try this:

   ▶ Say your multiplication tables in your head

   ▶ Count backward from 30 to 1

   ▶ Think about the last time you were really bored

   ▶ Most of all, do not think about what the other person did or said to you

3. Remember that you are giving control to the other person if you respond. Doing nothing means that you win and they lose because you stayed in control.

   Plan for the next time this same person tries to get to you. Remember that there will be a next time. People who like to push the buttons of others usually try again and the second and third time it might be worse. When it happens, remind yourself that

   ▶ It Gets Worse Before It Gets Better

   ▶ Winning Is Not Who Is Best at Put-Downs

   ▶ Winning Is Taking Care of Your Own Emotions

Pushing Your Buttons

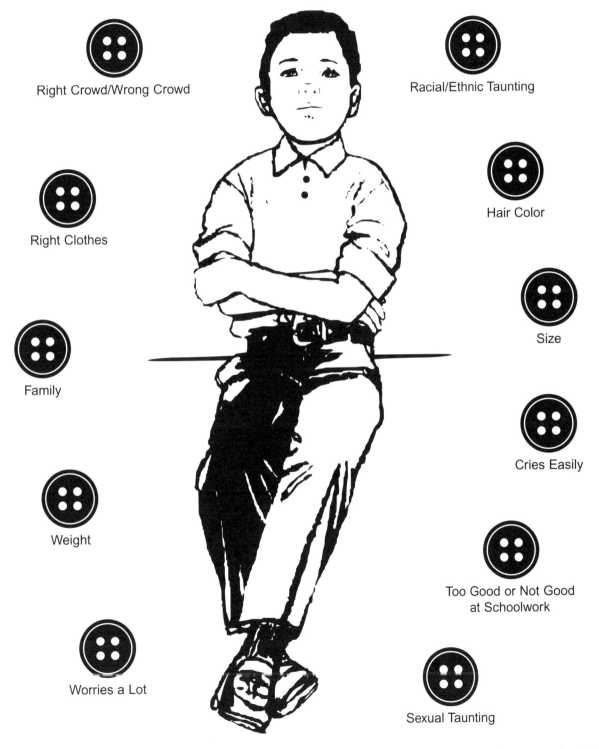

Right Crowd/Wrong Crowd

Racial/Ethnic Taunting

Right Clothes

Hair Color

Family

Size

Weight

Cries Easily

Worries a Lot

Too Good or Not Good
at Schoolwork

Sexual Taunting

HA HA, SO Shield

HA HA, SO

Help   **A**ssert Yourself

Humor   **A**void

Self-Talk   **O**wn

Practicing Strategies for the Victims

MATERIALS

Handout 19: First/Second Grade Role Play—Female

Handout 20: First/Second Grade Role Play—Male

Handout 21: Third/Fourth Grade Role Play—Female

Handout 22: Third/Fourth Grade Role Play—Male

Handout 23: Fifth/Sixth Grade Role Play—Female

Handout 24: Fifth/Sixth Grade Role Play—Male

OBJECTIVES

To have the students practice the strategies that they learned to use when they are being victimized by a bully.

STEPS

1. **Last Lesson Review**
   Ask the students to recall what HA HA, SO stands for.

2. **Role Play**
   Ask the children to each write one bullying incident that they have either experienced or witnessed on an index card or piece of paper. (If for some reason the children are unable to generate any scenarios, sample role plays are provided—see *Handouts 19* through 24.) Select a few of the children's scenarios to role play that are representative of both typical male and female bullying tactics. Be sure to include at least one example of a provocative victim.

For each role play scenario, ask for student volunteers to play the bully and the victim. As the rest of the class watches quietly, direct the volunteers in performing the role plays appropriately (using one or more of the HA HA, SO strategies). After each role play, have the whole class discuss the role play scenario and identify the strategy or strategies used by the victim.

Facilitator Notes

It is important to allow the students to **volunteer** for performing the role play parts, as students who are actual victims of bullying may find enacting bully-victim incidents before the class too emotionally charged. If the majority of the students appear to find the role playing uncomfortable or intimidating, an alternate method of enacting the bully-victim situations is through puppet play. Using puppets (available in any toy store) sometimes distances the students from the roles they are playing and allows them to more easily "speak through the character."

Sample Role Plays

You are a student in first or second grade. A group of girls leaves out one girl and won't let her play. Finally she finds a friend to play with one recess, and the other girls go over to the playmate and say, "Why would you want to play with her?" (This role play is found in *Handout 19.*)

You are a student in first or second grade. You notice that a couple of boys constantly make fun of another boy who is artistic. They tease him and call him a "sissy." They invite him to play kickball, although they know he doesn't like to play. After they encourage him to play, they leave him out or pick him last for their team. (This role play is found in *Handout 20*.)

You are a student in third or fourth grade. A new girl has just joined your class. She moved to your town from another state. Although she is pretty, she uses expressions and mannerisms that sound and seem different. A group of girls begin to mimic her way of talking and gesturing. They especially laugh and make fun of her at lunch time, refusing to leave a place for her at the table. (This role play is found in *Handout 21*.)

You are a student in third or fourth grade. One boy in your class has a learning disability and leaves the classroom each morning to go to a resource class for help with reading. Boys in your class call him "Stupid." Other boys call him at home and ask for "the dumb kid." One day, some boys take his special reading book and toss it back and forth on the playground, saying, "See if you can get anything right now, you dummy." (This role play is found in *Handout 22*.)

You are a student in fifth or sixth grade. A couple of girls have been picking on one of your classmates. They have been spreading rumors that she has an older boyfriend in high school. They wrote fake notes to her from this boyfriend with things about sex in them. Then they showed these notes to other girls. Now no one wants to be that girl's friend. (This role play is found in *Handout 23*.)

You are a student in fifth or sixth grade. One boy in your class whose parents are getting a divorce is in an angry mood a lot. He has gotten into some minor physical fights with other boys.

Lately he seems to be going after one particular boy. He trips him in the halls and runs into him at recess. Then he calls him "Clumsy" or says, "Why don't you watch where you are going?" (This role play is found in *Handout 24*.)

Optional Activity

Using Handouts 16, 17, and 18 (from the previous lesson), students can discuss which buttons of the victim were being pushed by the bully in each role play. Furthermore, which HA HA, SO strategies would be most effective can be discussed.

NEXT LESSON

In the next lesson, strategies for the students to use as "helpers" in the classroom are presented. These are techniques that "the caring majority" (discussed in the previous chapter) of students (the 85% of students who are neither bullies nor victims) can employ to assist the victims and prevent bullying behavior.

First/Second Grade Role Play—Female

You are a student in first or second grade. A group of girls leaves out one girl and won't let her play. Finally she finds a friend to play with one recess, and the other girls go over to the playmate and say, "Why would you want to play with her?"

Discussion Questions

1. How could the victim use each of the following HA HA, SO strategies?

   ▶ Help

   ▶ Assert Yourself

   ▶ Humor

   ▶ Avoid

   ▶ Self-Talk

   ▶ Own It

2. Which is the best strategy to try first?

3. Which is the best strategy to try second?

4. Is there any strategy the victim would be wise not to try?

First/Second Grade Role Play—Male

You are a student in first or second grade. You notice that a couple of boys constantly make fun of another boy who is artistic. They tease him and call him a "sissy." They invite him to play kickball, although they know he doesn't like to play. After they encourage him to play, they leave him out or pick him last for their team.

Discussion Questions

1. How could the victim use each of the following HA HA, SO strategies?

   ▶ Help

   ▶ Assert Yourself

   ▶ Humor

   ▶ Avoid

   ▶ Self-Talk

   ▶ Own It

2. Which is the best strategy to try first?

3. Which is the best strategy to try second?

4. Is there any strategy the victim would be wise not to try?

Third/Fourth Grade Role Play—Female

You are a student in third or fourth grade. A new girl has just joined your class. She moved to your town from another state. Although she is pretty, she uses expressions and mannerisms that sound and seem different. A group of girls begin to mimic her way of talking and gesturing. They especially laugh and make fun of her at lunch time, refusing to leave a place for her at the table.

Discussion Questions

1. How could the victim use each of the following HA HA, SO strategies?

   ▶ Help

   ▶ Assert Yourself

   ▶ Humor

   ▶ Avoid

   ▶ Self-Talk

   ▶ Own It

2. Which is the best strategy to try first?

3. Which is the best strategy to try second?

4. Is there any strategy the victim would be wise not to try?

Third/Fourth Grade Role Play—Male

You are a student in third or fourth grade. One boy in your class has a learning disability and leaves the classroom each morning to go to a resource class for help with reading. Boys in your class call him "Stupid." Other boys call him at home and ask for "the dumb kid." One day, some boys take his special reading book and toss it back and forth on the playground, saying, "See if you can get anything right now, you dummy."

Discussion Questions

1. How could the victim use each of the following HA HA, SO strategies?

   ▶ Help

   ▶ Assert Yourself

   ▶ Humor

   ▶ Avoid

   ▶ Self-Talk

   ▶ Own It

2. Which is the best strategy to try first?

3. Which is the best strategy to try second?

4. Is there any strategy the victim would be wise not to try?

Fifth/Sixth Grade Role Play—Female

You are a student in fifth or sixth grade. A couple of girls have been picking on one of your classmates. They have been spreading rumors that she has an older boyfriend in high school. They wrote fake notes to her from this boyfriend with things about sex in them. Then they showed these notes to other girls. Now no one wants to be that girl's friend.

Discussion Questions

1. How could the victim use each of the following HA HA, SO strategies?

   ▶ Help

   ▶ Assert Yourself

   ▶ Humor

   ▶ Avoid

   ▶ Self-Talk

   ▶ Own It

2. Which is the best strategy to try first?

3. Which is the best strategy to try second?

4. Is there any strategy the victim would be wise not to try?

Fifth/Sixth Grade Role Play—Male

You are a student in fifth or sixth grade. One boy in your class whose parents are getting a divorce is in an angry mood a lot. He has gotten into some minor physical fights with other boys.

Lately he seems to be going after one particular boy. He trips him in the halls and runs into him at recess. Then he calls him "Clumsy" or says, "Why don't you watch where you are going?"

Discussion Questions

1. How could the victim use each of the following HA HA, SO strategies?

   ▶ Help

   ▶ Assert Yourself

   ▶ Humor

   ▶ Avoid

   ▶ Self-Talk

   ▶ Own It

2. Which is the best strategy to try first?

3. Which is the best strategy to try second?

4. Is there any strategy the victim would be wise not to try?

Teaching Strategies for the Helpers

MATERIALS

Poster 25: CARES

Handout 26: What I Can Do IF . . .

OBJECTIVES

To present strategies for the students to use as "helpers" in the classroom. These "CARES" strategies are techniques that "the caring majority" of students (the 85% of students who are neither bullies nor victims) can employ to assist the victims and prevent bullying behavior.

STEPS

1. **Last Lesson Review**
   Check that the students still remember what HA HA, SO stands for.

2. **Group Activity**
   To expand upon the students' understanding of bullying situations and break the ice, read a story from your school's library or show a video that addresses a bully-victim situation that emphasizes the feelings of the victim. Be sure to select one that is appropriate to the age group of the children.

   After the story or video, lead a class discussion about how the victim character might have been feeling. Have the class brainstorm appropriate "feeling words," and write them on the board. Get them started with words like "scared," "lonely," "sad," "hurt," and "fearful."

   Encourage the students to develop compassion for the victim by making pointed statements and asking leading

questions, such as:

- ▶ "How many of you have ever had a similar thing happen to you?"

- ▶ "Feeling afraid is not a very nice feeling, is it?"

- ▶ "How does your body feel when you are scared?"

- ▶ "What does it feel like to be sad? Do you ever feel like crying when you are sad?"

- ▶ "Does everyone feel lonely sometimes? Can you remember the last time you felt lonely?"

Encourage the students to **think about their answers** to these questions. They will not have to raise their hands or answer out loud, to avoid embarrassment, but they can volunteer answers or feelings if they like.

3. **Teach and Model for the Students the CARES Strategies**
   Explain to the children that as part of their classroom rules against bullying, they will be expected to (and taught how to) help the victims of bullying (see *Poster 25*).

   CARES

   C – Creative Problem Solving
   A – Adult Help
   R – Relate and Join
   E – Empathy
   S – Stand Up and Speak Out

   - ▶ **Creative Problem Solving**—Teach the students how to address a bullying situation through creative problem solving.

RESOURCE GUIDE

See "Videotapes and Films for Students," "Books for Primary Students," or "Books for Intermediate Students" for materials that emphasize the feelings of the victim in bullying situations.

A helper can use this strategy by saying, for example, "It looks like you two have a problem and maybe I can help you solve it. Lisa, you've been giving Margaret put-downs so now you could even it out by giving her some build-ups."

▶ **Adult Help**—Teach the students when and how to seek help from an adult to keep things safe. Remind them about the difference between "tattling" and "telling" (see *Handout/ Poster 14*). Also remind students of the adult they named in Lesson 3 that they could get help from.

This strategy should be used when the "Stand Up and Speak Out" and "Creative Problem Solving" strategies are not working and especially when the helper feels scared too. The helper should seek out the teacher or another adult, explain the bullying situation and the strategies that have been tried, and ask for help.

▶ **Relate and Join**—Teach the students how to join with and support the victim. Remind them that "there is strength in numbers."

This strategy involves helping the victim by clarifying differences. If a learning-disabled student is called "dumb," for example, a helper could say, "We all have things we're good at and things we're not so good at. I'm not so good at being organized." With racial slurs, a helper might say, for example, "Jody is black and I'm glad. Think how boring our class would be if we were all white."

This helping strategy can be illustrated by historical examples of joining, e.g., King of Denmark putting on the Star of David when the Nazis arrived and demanded it of the Jews.

▶ **Empathy**—Teach the students how to empathize with feelings the victim might be experiencing. This strategy can involve simply telling a victim you felt with them after an observed bullying incident.

This strategy also can involve speaking out against bullying (the "Stand Up and Speak Out" strategy). A helper could say, for example, "Janet, you've been spreading rumors about Amy that aren't true. I don't like it and it is against our school rules. If I were Amy, I'd feel hurt, confused, and mad."

▶ **Stand Up and Speak Out**—Teach the students how to speak out against bullying (use *Handout 26*). A helper might say, "Juan, making fun of James' baggy sweater isn't nice. I have one almost like it at home and I think I'll wear it tomorrow because old, soft sweaters are so comfortable. You can wear one too if you want to."

Explain to the students that the first strategy that they try when helping a victim may not work. In that case, they will have to try another. That is why you are giving them five strategies and an easy way to remember them (CARES)—so that they will have lots of things to try. After they know the five strategies really well, they will be able to quickly figure out which strategy to try first, second, and so on, in each unique bullying situation.

As an indication of their understanding of these strategies, ask the class to identify the strategy or strategies used by the other characters (other than the bully and victim) in the story or video you presented to the class at the beginning of this session. If none of the CARES strategies were used, ask the students to identify the strategy or strategies that the other characters **should have** used to help the victim.

To reinforce the memorization of the CARES mnemonic, you may wish to have the students repeat the strategies in some way, such as singing CARES to a familiar tune, calling out the strategies as you yell the CARES "cheer" (e.g., "Give me a C!" "Creative Problem Solving!" "Give me an A!" "Adult Help!"), or by any other means you can think of that would be fun and memorable for the students.

Hang *Poster 25* up in the classroom with the other bullying posters to remind the students about the strategies they can use to help the victims of bullying.

Facilitator Notes

Be sure to present these strategies using examples relevant to the students' lives and experiences at school. This will assist the students in internalizing them.

NEXT LESSON

In the next lesson, the children will have the opportunity to try these strategies themselves, and practice them to a comfort level through role play.

CARES

What I Can Do if I See Someone Being Bullied

CARES

C   Creative Problem Solving

A   Adult Help

R   Relate and Join

E   Empathy

S   Stand Up and Speak Out

What I Can Do IF . . .

What I Can Do if I am Being Bullied

Help	Seek assistance from an adult, friend, or peer when a potentially threatening situation arises. Seek help also if other strategies aren't working. **Tips:** ▶ Brainstorm all of the sources of help at your school: counselors, teachers, nurse, parent, neighbor, or sibling. ▶ Stress the different ways to get help—anonymously, in a group, a school hotline.
Assert Yourself	Make assertive statements to the bully addressing your feelings about the bully's behavior. **Tips:** ▶ Best strategy for a victim to start with. ▶ Should not be used with severe bullying. ▶ Victim should look bully straight in the eye. ▶ Use "I" statement, ex. "I don't like that."
Humor	Use humor to de-escalate a situation. **Tips:** ▶ Use humor in a positive way. ▶ Make sure the joke is about what the bully said, not about the bully.
Avoid	Walk away or avoid certain places in order to avoid bullying. **Tips:** ▶ Best for situations when victim is alone. ▶ Avoid places where the bully hangs out. ▶ Join with others rather than be alone.
Self-Talk	Use positive self-talk to maintain positive self-esteem during a bullying situation. **Tips:** ▶ Use as a means to keep feeling good about yourself. ▶ Think positive statements about self and accomplishments. ▶ Rehearse mental strategies to avoid being hooked by the bully.
Own It	"Own" the put-down or belittling comment in order to diffuse it. **Tips:** ▶ Agree with the bully and leave the situation, such as, "OK" or "Thanks for the information." ▶ Combine with humor strategies, such as, "Yeah, this IS a bad haircut. The lawn mower got out of control this weekend." ▶ Combine with assertive strategies, such as, "Yes, I did fail the test and I don't appreciate you looking at my paper."

What I Can Do if I See Someone Being Bullied

Creative Problem Solving	Get involved in solving the problem of bullying. **Tips:** ◗ Say, "Can I help you solve the problem? Three heads are better than just two." ◗ Brainstorm solutions to the conflict, ex. how to share something, give build-ups after put-downs.
Adult Help	Get help from adults. **Tips:** ◗ This is the best strategy if the situation seems dangerous. ◗ Use this when other strategies aren't working. ◗ It is not tattling when you are trying to keep someone safe.
Relate and Join	Join with and support victims. **Tips:** ◗ Remember there is safety and strength in numbers. ◗ Invite a victim to play with your group. ◗ Go and stand by a victim who is being taunted and say, "I'm clumsy too." ◗ Give an explanation about a victim's behavior or say things you like about the victim.
Empathy	Try to understand the feelings of the victim and share that understanding. **Tips:** ◗ Give a victim support after you observed them being bullied by sharing your understanding. ◗ Combine with "Stand Up and Speak Out" such as saying to the bully, "That comment would have hurt my feelings, so I'm sure it hurt John."
Stand Up and Speak Out	Take a stand against bullying by speaking out when you see it occur. **Tips:** ◗ This is not a good strategy in a dangerous bullying situation. ◗ This is the most effective strategy to stop bullying and it requires courage. ◗ Say, "Don't make fun of her clothes. Bullying is not allowed at our school."

Practicing Strategies for the Helpers

MATERIALS

Handout 27: First Grade Role Play

Handout 28: Second Grade Role Play

Handout 29: Third Grade Role Play

Handout 30: Fourth Grade Role Play

Handout 31: Fifth Grade Role Play

Handout 32: Sixth Grade Role Play

Handout 33: CARES Buttons

OBJECTIVES

To have the students practice the strategies that they learned to use to help the victims of bullying, to introduce a weekly reinforcement program for caring behavior ("I Caught You Caring").

STEPS

1. **Last Lesson Review**
   Ask the students to recall what CARES stands for.

2. **Role Play**
   Ask the students to each write one bullying incident that they have witnessed on an index card or piece of paper. (If for some reason the students are unable to generate any scenarios, sample role plays are provided—see *Handouts 27 through 32.*) Select a few of the students' scenarios to role play that are representative of both typical male and female bullying tactics. Be sure to include at least one example with a provocative victim.

For each role play scenario, ask for student volunteers to play the bully, the victim, and the "helper." As the rest of the class watches quietly, direct the volunteers in performing the role plays appropriately (using one or more of the CARES strategies). After each role play, have the whole class discuss the role play scenario and identify the strategy or strategies used by the helper.

Facilitator Notes

If the majority of the students appear to find the role playing uncomfortable or intimidating, an alternate method of enacting the bully-victim situations is through puppet play. Using puppets (available in any toy store) sometimes distances the students from the roles they are playing and allows them to more easily "speak through the character."

Sample Role Plays

Besides role plays, the following six scenarios can be used in a variety of ways:

▶ You could read a scenario aloud and then have the class vote on the different alternatives, followed by some classroom discussion.

▶ You could hand these out individually and ask each student to read them alone and to indicate the alternative(s) he or she prefers.

▶ You could then collect them and without revealing names, share with the class the different alternatives that the most students voted for.

▶ With the intermediate grade levels that have reading and writing skills, you could ask the students to complete them on their own as an assignment and to hand them in for discussion during the next session.

One Friday you overhear Lauren, a bossy, know-it-all girl who sits next to you, tell another girl in your class, Tamara, "I bet you got an 'F' again on your spelling test." You notice that Tamara looks like she is about to cry. Tamara often looks sad and you know that she is not a very good student, but she is nice and you like her. (This role play is found in *Handout 27.*)

You are on a class field trip to the zoo with a fifth grade class. You notice three of the fifth grade boys making fun of Jerold, a boy in your class, because he is having trouble filling out his question and answer sheet about the animals. You look around for a parent or teacher to do something and you can't find any adult to help Jerold.

Later in the morning, your group meets with the rest of the class for lunch. Jerold is missing and does not come for lunch. You feel very worried about him. (This role play is found in *Handout 28.*)

At recess, a lot of the children like to play a game called "Capture." Sometimes Jane doesn't like to play because running a lot is difficult for her. This particular day Jane decides to play and sure enough, she gets captured right away. The captors call her "slow, slimy snail" and take her to "The Dungeon." They tell her to clean all the crab apples off all the other captured children's shoes before she can be released. You can tell she feels angry and doesn't want to do it. You feel scared and worried for Jane.

Finally the bell rings and recess is over. You feel so relieved and happy to go back into class. All through the afternoon, you keep thinking about what happened and worrying about the next recess. You aren't certain what to do.

(This role play is found in *Handout 29.*)

You usually play with Brent at recess. In fact, Brent is probably one of your best friends. One day you end up playing soccer with some of the other kids instead of playing with Brent. He doesn't mind because he has other friends too.

During the soccer game, you look over and see Brent in a fist fight with Mitchell. Brent doesn't ever play with Mitchell, but they live in the same neighborhood and ride the bus together so you know they know each other. You've never seen Brent fight before and you are really surprised. (This role play is found in *Handout 30.*)

You have known for a long time that there is a secret club of girls in your room. The three girls who run it are bossy and pretty mean. They scare you a lot of the time and you just avoid them. They have never picked on you and you are thankful.

One day you are walking into class when you hear them calling Leah, an African-American girl who is new, a really nasty name. You feel upset and sorry for Leah, who seems pretty nice to you. Plus you know that putting someone down for their skin color is wrong and unfair. (This role play is found in *Handout 31.*)

Your school has a new program this year. Every morning a group of eight students meets with a teacher advisor to talk about school issues and feelings. You don't really like these meetings and usually you just keep quiet and listen. One morning about five of the other kids start complaining about a boy named Jonathan. They say that he is always a pest. He stands too close to them, bothers them when they are working, and won't play games by the rules. He gets in fights all the time with Chris and the other kids give the impression that Jonathan is the one who starts the fights.

Because you are quiet and watch others a lot, you know that what they are reporting is not quite how it all happens. You agree that Jonathan is a pest, but you also know that Chris is really a bully and the one who starts the fights. Jonathan is just easy for Chris to pick on because he is always pestering others. In fact, you have seen Chris do some really mean things, like write bad names inside Jonathan's locker and threaten him out of money and things in his lunch. You feel like someone needs to tell the advisor the truth about Chris. (This role play is found in *Handout 32.*)

3. **Introduce the "I Caught You Caring" Reinforcement Program**
Now that the students are familiar with and comfortable about performing the caring behaviors of a "helper," let them know that the best helper each week will be rewarded.

Explain to the students what will happen in the "I Caught You Caring" sessions each week, when these classroom sessions will take place, and what the special reward will be.

I Caught You Caring
These weekly sessions are designed for reinforcement of caring behavior within the classroom. They occur at the end of the week (e.g., Friday before dismissal), and take approximately five to fifteen minutes.

Each teacher chooses one of his or her students who he or she "caught" being kind or helpful to another student for this special recognition. The teacher should keep a log of "acts of kindness" that he or she notices during the week, and then pick a good example to reinforce.

During the session, the teacher should announce the "Caring Student of the Week" and describe the caring behavior that he or she performed. The teacher should discuss with the class why the behavior worked/how it complied with the classroom rules, and model the

skill(s) for the students. Some brief discussion can then occur about what motivated the caring behavior.

Note: These class discussions can be expanded upon and enlivened, if you wish, by employing creative discussion techniques. For example, you could read *Finding the Greenstone*, by Alice Walker, to your class, and then allow the children to pass a green marble among themselves as they are "caught caring."

Also explain to the students that when they have all become very good helpers, who perform the caring behaviors almost all the time, they will be able to nominate and vote for the student with the "Best Caring Behavior" each week. When appropriate, explain that program and the special reward (the "CARES Buttons," *Handout 33*).

RESOURCE GUIDE

See "Books for Primary Students" for complete information on Alice Walker's book.

NEXT LESSON

In the next lesson, all the skills presented in the classroom curriculum will be reviewed and reinforced for the students.

First Grade Role Play

One Friday you overhear Lauren, a bossy, know-it-all girl who sits next to you, tell another girl in your class, Tamara, "I bet you got an 'F' again on your spelling test." You notice that Tamara looks like she is about to cry. Tamara often looks sad and you know that she is not a very good student, but she is nice and you like her.

1. How could the helper use each of the following CARES strategies?

   a. Creative Problem Solving

   b. Adult Help

   c. Relate and Join

   d. Empathy

   e. Stand Up and Speak Out

2. Which is the best strategy to try first?

3. Which is the best strategy to try second?

4. Is there any strategy the helper would be wise not to try?

Second Grade Role Play

You are on a class field trip to the zoo with your second grade class and a fifth grade class. You notice three of the fifth grade boys making fun of Jerold, a boy in your class, because he is having trouble filling out his question and answer sheet about the animals. You look around for a parent or teacher to do something and you can't find any adult to help Jerold.

Later in the morning, your group meets with the rest of the class for lunch. Jerold is missing and does not come for lunch. You feel very worried about him.

1. How could the helper use each of the following CARES strategies?

   a. Creative Problem Solving

   b. Adult Help

   c. Relate and Join

   d. Empathy

   e. Stand Up and Speak Out

2. Which is the best strategy to try first?

3. Which is the best strategy to try second?

4. Is there any strategy the helper would be wise not to try?

Third Grade Role Play

At recess, a lot of the children like to play a game called "Capture." Sometimes Jane doesn't like to play because running a lot is difficult for her. This particular day Jane decides to play and sure enough, she gets captured right away. The captors call her "slow, slimy snail" and take her to "The Dungeon." They tell her to clean all the crab apples off all the other captured children's shoes before she can be released. You can tell she feels angry and doesn't want to do it. You feel scared and worried for Jane.

Finally the bell rings and recess is over. You feel so relieved and happy to go back into class. All through the afternoon, you keep thinking about what happened and worrying about the next recess. You aren't certain what to do.

1. How could the helper use each of the following CARES strategies?

   a. Creative Problem Solving

   b. Adult Help

   c. Relate and Join

   d. Empathy

   e. Stand Up and Speak Out

2. Which is the best strategy to try first?

3. Which is the best strategy to try second?

4. Is there any strategy the helper would be wise not to try?

Fourth Grade Role Play

You usually play with Brent at recess. In fact, Brent is probably one of your best friends. One day you end up playing soccer with some of the other kids instead of playing with Brent. He doesn't mind because he has other friends too.

During the soccer game, you look over and see Brent in a fist fight with Mitchell. Brent doesn't ever play with Mitchell, but they live in the same neighborhood and ride the bus together so you know they know each other. You've never seen Brent fight before and you are really surprised.

1. How could the helper use each of the following CARES strategies?

   a. Creative Problem Solving

   b. Adult Help

   c. Relate and Join

   d. Empathy

   e. Stand Up and Speak Out

2. Which is the best strategy to try first?

3. Which is the best strategy to try second?

4. Is there any strategy the helper would be wise not to try?

Fifth Grade Role Play

You have known for a long time that there is a secret club of girls in your room. The three girls who run it are bossy and pretty mean. They scare you a lot of the time and you just avoid them. They have never picked on you and you are thankful.

One day you are walking into class when you hear them calling Leah, an African-American girl who is new, a really nasty name. You feel upset and sorry for Leah, who seems pretty nice to you. Plus you know that putting someone down for their skin color is wrong and unfair.

1. How could the helper use each of the following CARES strategies?

    a. Creative Problem Solving

    b. Adult Help

    c. Relate and Join

    d. Empathy

    e. Stand Up and Speak Out

2. Which is the best strategy to try first?

3. Which is the best strategy to try second?

4. Is there any strategy the helper would be wise not to try?

Sixth Grade Role Play

Your school has a new program this year. Every morning a group of eight students meets with a teacher advisor to talk about school issues and feelings. You don't really like these meetings and usually you just keep quiet and listen. One morning about five of the other kids start complaining about a boy named Jonathan. They say that he is always a pest. He stands too close to them, bothers them when they are working, and won't play games by the rules. He gets in fights all the time with Chris and the other kids give the impression that Jonathan is the one who starts the fights.

Because you are quiet and watch others a lot, you know that what they are reporting is not quite how it all happens. You agree that Jonathan is a pest, but you also know that Chris is really a bully and the one who starts the fights. Jonathan is just easy for Chris to pick on because he is always pestering others. In fact, you have seen Chris do some really mean things, like write bad names inside Jonathan's locker and threaten him out of money and things in his lunch. You feel like someone needs to tell the advisor the truth about Chris.

1. How could the helper use each of the following CARES strategies?

   a. Creative Problem Solving

   b. Adult Help

   c. Relate and Join

   d. Empathy

   e. Stand Up and Speak Out

2. Which is the best strategy to try first?

3. Which is the best strategy to try second?

4. Is there any strategy the helper would be wise not to try?

CARES Buttons

I performed a daring act of

KINDNESS

I make a
great friend.

I CARE!

I am
a Kind,
Caring
Kid!

KINDNESS S★T★A★R

Note: These "buttons" are designed to be photocopied, cut out, and inserted into two popular sizes of pin style name badges (convention size: 4" x 3" or 3.5" x 2.25"), available in most office supply stores.

Follow-Up
Review Lesson

MATERIALS

Refer back to any handouts/posters from Lesson 1-6 relating to skills to reinforce and review, including:

Handout/Poster 10: Classroom Rules

Poster 15: HA HA, SO

Poster 25: CARES

OBJECTIVES

To revisit the classroom three to six weeks after the classroom curriculum was taught to: (1) evaluate student progress and determine whether any new bullying problems have surfaced; (2) review and reinforce the student skills to prevent bullying behavior and reinforce positive caring skills, and (3) provide any additional instruction necessary to ensure the continued success of the program.

STEPS

1. **Evaluation of Student Progress**
   Before the review lesson, discuss with the classroom teacher his or her perceptions of student progress. Find out whether any new problems have surfaced in the classroom and/or observations of positive changes.

2. **Reteach Any Skills Specifically Related to Any Problems Identified in the Class Discussion**
   Based on the results of the readministered survey, reteach all or applicable parts of the sessions addressing deficient skills.

3. **Conclude the Session**
   Summarize for the students that they have learned some important things: (1) what they can do if a bully picks on them, (2) what to do if they see a bully picking on someone else, (3) there is strength in numbers, and (4) how kind and caring acts can become contagious. Remind them that they will have to keep practicing these strategies to get good at them and that their teacher will be available to help them if they have any questions or need help practicing.

   Remind the students that the rules against bullying will stay posted and in effect. **No bullying will be allowed.** Tell students that the weekly "I Caught You Caring" sessions will continue through the school year.

Chapter Four

Creating and Maintaining the Caring Majority

The foundation and backbone of bully-proofing is developing the climate of the school into one where everyone sets a tone of caring and carries the message, "Our school will be a safe, respectful, and inclusive environment so teachers can teach and children can learn." The key to creating this climate is shifting the "silent majority" into a "caring majority."

The silent majority consists of the 85% of students who are neither bullies nor victims but who stand helplessly by as their classmates get beaten up emotionally or physically. By doing so, the bystander children are implicitly allowing this to happen. Empowering the silent majority reduces the fear bullies create. Children will report bullying if they know that the staff will intervene effectively. The silent majority knows who the bullies and victims are, but they are too frightened to intervene. The children in the younger grades, second and third especially, are eager and willing to lend their support to solving the problem as long as they feel protected. The influence of this silent majority is a powerful resource and a key to the success of the program.

Developing the intervention skills of the silent majority and turning them into a caring majority is crucial in setting a positive tone in a school. These students give strength and support to the victims and defuse the power of the bullies. The caring majority, along with responsive adults, is the most powerful resource in creating a safe and caring school environment.

Developing and Maintaining a Caring Majority

The caring majority is developed by mobilizing the silent majority to join together in shifting the atmosphere of fear and intimidation, which is created by the bullies, to an atmosphere of care and concern. Children remain silent out of fear. They are afraid that no one else feels as frightened as they do, they are afraid that the bullies will retaliate and harm them if they speak up, and they also are afraid that the staff and teachers will not take their side and protect them. Because of these fears, the caring majority cannot be unified until the underlying issues are addressed. The staff must be trained and ready to take action. They must communicate to the students that a "No Bullying" policy is in place and will be enforced. The classroom curriculum sessions need to be completed. These teach the students that they are not alone, what bullying behavior is, why telling is different from tattling, how to protect themselves from bullying, and how to intervene in caring ways against bullying. After these steps have been taken, the students are ready to be mobilized into forming a caring majority in their school environment.

The caring majority must be developed comprehensively at the individual and classroom levels and throughout the school as a whole. This is implemented through the following four guiding principles (Identifying the Behaviors and Characteristics of a Caring Community, Recognizing and Reinforcing Caring Majority Behaviors, Developing Classroom

Guiding Principles for the Development of the Caring School Community

Guiding Principle 1: Identifying the Behaviors and Characteristics of a Caring Community

▶ Identify behaviors and characteristics of a caring community member in your school.

▶ Identify school rules and expectations.

▶ Identify and teach the necessary skills.

▶ Develop and empower the courage to act (take a stand for caring behaviors).

Guiding Principle 2: Recognizing and Reinforcing Caring Majority Behaviors

▶ Identify and acknowledge students for displaying characteristics of a caring community member.

▶ Implement classroom-wide and school-wide acknowledgement plans.

Guiding Principle 3: Developing Classroom and School-wide Caring Majority Groups

▶ Establish and implement process to develop "caring majority" of students in classrooms.

▶ Design collateral school-wide activities to reinforce development of the caring majority throughout the school.

Guiding Principle 4: Using Teachable Moments

▶ Turn opportunities into teachable moments to reinforce concepts of the caring community.

▶ Use principles of the caring community in daily problem solving.

▶ Conduct weekly classroom meetings to develop and expand concepts.

and School-Wide Caring Majority Groups, and Using Teachable Moments). These principles are global concepts to be developed by your staff. A variety of effective techniques are described in the following principles. These are ideas for creative thinking among your staff. There are many avenues to developing the caring majority. Use the guiding principles as your goal while developing techniques that fit your school environment.

Guiding Principle One

Identifying the Behaviors and Characteristics of a Caring Community
Most children fall into the category of bystanders. These children make up the silent majority. They are not targeted nor

are they bullies, but they do suffer. Bystander children know the dynamics of the social setting and often report guilt later for not standing up to the bully on behalf of the victim or for joining the bully when they knew the behavior was wrong. They may worry that they will be the next victim if they fail to join in. Developing classroom-wide caring majority groups allows a bystander child the opportunity to not stand alone and to be an important part of changing the climate through a group process.

Techniques

▶ Identifying the Behaviors and Characteristics of a Caring Community

▶ Identifying the Rules and Expectations

▶ Identifying the Necessary Skills

▶ Finding the Courage to Act

Identifying the Behaviors and Characteristics of a Caring Community

With this technique students are encouraged to identify the behaviors and characteristics of a caring community. For example, a teacher may engage students in a discussion of caring behaviors and how they might treat others by having them generate a list of those qualities that define a caring person. The teacher can help the students by pointing out that caring can be based on many things:

▶ age

▶ unique qualities

▶ issues within the classroom

▶ world events

▶ diversity in class

▶ diversity in the community

For example, a caring person might:

▶ share

▶ know when to stop

▶ be helpful

▶ be fair

▶ have courage

▶ have a sense of humor

▶ be generous

▶ be aware of other's feelings

Here are two sample classroom lists that illustrate these characteristics.

A third grade classroom developed this list:

▶ caring and kind

▶ good student—responsible

▶ being nice to everyone

▶ sharing and including and inviting

▶ knowing when to stop

▶ helpful

▶ generous

▶ funny

▶ fair

▶ treat others like you would like to be treated

▶ participate and listen

▶ courage

A fourth grade classroom offered this list:

▶ friendly to everyone

▶ helpful

▶ not selfish

▶ sense of humor

▶ courage

▶ honesty

▶ consistent

▶ popular by liking everyone

▶ can think for themselves

▶ dependable

Identifying the Rules and Expectations

Once the behaviors and characteristics have been identified, students find it important to know that the adults in their school will be responsive. Clear rules and expectations from the adults are critical. But, in order for students to accept ownership for the rules and expectations in their classroom, they must feel that they are fair and that they have the ability to help make their school safe.

Point out to your students that rules define the behaviors you **do not** want students to do, but expectations define the behaviors that you **do** want students to do.

The following chart (with your classroom rules, consequences, and expectations) can be shown and discussed with the students in your classroom.

(Note: The students do not make the rules or the expectations but they can contribute ideas to gain ownership.)

Clear Rules and Expectations

RULES

What you **do not** want students to do:

- Fighting
- Running in hall
- Abusive language or harassment

EXPECTATIONS

What you **do** want students to do:

- Students will get adult help when needed.
- Students will treat others in a respectful manner.

CONSEQUENCES

What will happen to students:

- Automatic suspension
- You will go back and walk
- In-school suspension

- Students will include others.
- Students are at school to be learners.

Rules and expectations need to be reviewed and revised on a regular basis. It is recommended that this be done at least two times a year.

Identifying the Necessary Skills

Finally, the students need skills. While these have been developed during the classroom sessions in the previous chapter, the following chart illustrates additional ideas for discussion in the classroom.

Skills

HOW TO GET ADULT HELP

Have students work on these for themselves.

- What are the characteristics of adults from whom you would choose to get help?
- Who are three adults you can say anything to?

HOW TO JOIN TOGETHER WITH OTHERS TO STAND UP FOR WHAT IS RIGHT

- Who can you ask?
- How would you support one another?

FEELING EMPATHY FOR OTHER STUDENTS

- What would help you see others' opinions?

- Who has some of the same worries that you have?

HOW TO MEDIATE CONFLICTS WITH OTHER STUDENTS

- Identify the problem.
- Brainstorm the solutions.
- Self-regulate, i.e., stop yourself when you are reacting or out of control.
- Use self-protective skills so others can't push your buttons. Learn your buttons. Learn HA HA, SO. Identify what works for you.
- Learn to disengage when others are trying to push your buttons.

Finding the Courage to Act

Standing up for another child involves both risk and courage. Risk means the danger a child senses in a given situation. This varies from child to child; what is risky for one child may feel safe for another and each child deserves the right to determine his or her own sense of risk. Some children will take greater personal risks than others.

Courage is the decision to act. Any level of courage in helping another child is worthwhile. Doing something is better than doing nothing. Sometimes after just one child stands up for what is fair others will then be able to risk joining in. This is a critical part of forming the caring majority. Keeping in mind that no child should be pushed into an action he or she is not ready to take, all children should be encouraged to think about this concept: **"What is the risk for me?"** The following are a few activities to get you started:

1. Ask each child in your classroom to think of three things he or she has seen in the movies or on television that were courageous. Then ask the children to think of three things seen in your school or community that were courageous. Present *Handout 34* to the students.

2. Present the five different strategies to the class.

   For children in the younger grades, use the metaphor of a giraffe and a turtle. A giraffe is an animal that sticks its neck "way out" and a turtle is an animal that "hides." Everyone is encouraged to be a giraffe but some may have longer necks than others. Ask each child, "How far can you stick out your neck?"

   For older students, ask, "How much courage does it take?" to do the following: (Assign each situation a number from one to ten, with ten being the lowest.)

   ‣ How much courage does it take to tell someone his or her shoelace is untied?

   ‣ How much courage does it take to ask someone new if he or she would like to sit with you at lunch?

   ‣ How much courage does it take to say "hello" to a student in a higher grade?

   ‣ How much courage does it take to walk over to someone who is bullying and say, "We don't treat people like that at this school"?

   ‣ How much courage does it take to tell the victim that you saw what happened and it was not fair?

   Review the idea that doing something is better than doing nothing by telling students, "Don't be a silent bystander. Do something to join the caring majority."

   Children who have the courage to stand up to the bully, at some level of risk, build their own character in the process of helping someone else. Often they are noticed by other children and adults and admired and recognized for their willingness to do something. This process starts in the classroom and then moves school-wide.

   Thus, students are taught that caring majority behaviors exist on a continuum from lower level behaviors, such as picking up a pencil that someone has dropped, to more courageous behaviors such as including a child who has been left out or rejected by other children, at the risk of being rejected as well. While words such as respect, kindness, and caring are important concepts, they are vague and not very useful for teaching children what specific behaviors are expected. Furthermore, the lower-level behaviors are important building blocks for later behaviors, and likely play a more important role in early elementary grades than in the later elementary grades. Caring respectful behaviors must be defined.

3. Review the "Strategies of Intervention Chart" once a month using at least three examples of courageous behaviors. Draw examples from your own

classroom, school or community, or generate your own. The following examples will help you get started:

▶ **Lower Level (courteous behaviors)**

- Saying, "Thank You," "Please," and "Excuse Me"

- Picking up an item dropped by another person

- Standing quietly in line

- Waiting one's turn while talking

- Apologizing for a mistake

- Giving a person a compliment

- Doing a favor for someone

- Allowing another child to play when he or she asks

▶ **Middle Level (courageous and caring behaviors)**

- Sticking up for a friend

- Refusing to join in when someone is being treated badly (e.g., being teased)

- Not spreading a rumor that is told to you

▶ **Higher Level (very courageous and caring behaviors)**

- Getting adult assistance during a bully situation

- Making an effort to assist a child who is rejected or lonely (e.g., asking her to play, or helping out in a potentially embarrassing situation)

- Stopping the spread of a rumor

- Sticking up for a person whom you don't know very well

- Saying, "We don't treat people like that at our school."

Guiding Principle Two

Recognizing and Reinforcing Caring Majority Behaviors

Caring majority behaviors need to be reinforced. After the students have developed a classroom list of caring majority behaviors and characteristics, the teacher must immediately start modeling these behaviors. In addition, children who display these characteristics are identified and praised. Use weekly reinforcement and acknowledgment by developing celebrations that are non-competitive and celebrate the act, not just the person. Practice "I Caught You Caring" as described in the classroom sessions in the previous chapter or use some of the following reinforcers:

▶ Verbal praise

▶ Classroom-wide acknowledgment:

- Classroom praise

- Phone call to parents to acknowledge the caring behavior

- Picking a "Caring student of the week"

- Giving out Caring tickets for an end of the month raffle

▶ Using the "Caring Majority Recognition Form": Students caught performing a caring act receive a recognition slip (see *Handout 35*).

The names of students who receive a caring recognition slip are placed on a bulletin board in a public part of the school.

The names of students who receive a caring recognition slip are read over the intercom at the end of the week. A certificate of appreciation is sent home (see *Handout 36*).

▶ Earning a special privilege:

- extra recess

- a trip to the library

- a gift certificate for the school store

- a field trip or lunch with the teacher or aide

Guiding Principle Three

Developing Classroom and School-Wide Caring Majority Groups

It is important to hold regular (i.e., weekly) classroom meetings to create and maintain a caring community at the classroom level. Teachers conducting classroom meetings need to remind students of expected caring behaviors and allow time to debrief bullying events in a safe and caring manner. It is also a time to review bully-proofing skills and strategies as well as to applaud individual and group successes. Holding a regular caring majority meeting can help solidify these ideas.

Some possible ideas for your meetings might include:

▶ Creating a caring jungle with each child's name on an animal that is placed in the jungle as he or she demonstrates caring majority behaviors.

▶ Creating a rainbow with the student's names placed on the rainbow as they work toward the pot of gold at the end of the rainbow. Movement along the rainbow is based on caring behaviors.

▶ Creating a tree and each student's name is on a leaf.

▶ "Tattling" on good behavior. (Each week call on three to four students and ask them to "tattle on someone he or she saw doing a caring act.)

▶ Giving each student a card and instructing them to write one name on the card. Give the following instruction, "write the name of the person who is the most different from you for whatever reason." Next the teacher collects the cards. After the cards are collected, the teacher then gives the following instructions: "This week do one kind, courteous, or thoughtful act for the person named on your card."

The following week, each student tells whose name was on the card and what he or she did. Also discuss how the recipient of the caring behavior responded.

▶ Playing the "gather together circle game."

Have students line up along each of 4 circles you have created in blue, red, green, and yellow with:

• everyone who feels they stuck out their neck for someone else this week standing on the blue circle

• everyone who gave a compliment to someone this week standing on the red circle

• everyone who saw bullying but felt afraid to do anything standing on the green circle

• everyone who heard a put down this week standing on the yellow circle

(This game creates a visual image of the caring majority besides being fun to participate in.)

▶ Creating a "compliment" bulletin board. Have the students name possible ways to give a compliment. Write them on cards and post them on a board as a reminder of how to give a compliment.

Identification Model

The following model requires expertise and experience in running groups for children. Please proceed with due consideration.

After developing a class list of Caring Majority behaviors, students are identified who consistently exemplify these behaviors. The teacher models the nomination process by identifying a student who shows caring majority behavior. The teacher then gives examples of the nominee's positive behavior.

The teacher asks students for their feedback regarding the appropriateness of the nomination, as well. In subsequent weekly meetings the teacher (or facilitator) asks students for additional nominations. Nominations need to be supported by examples of caring behaviors. Sometimes bullies are nominated to be part of the

What a Caring Community Can Do

▶ Create a safe, respectful, inclusive environment so teachers can teach and students can learn

▶ Provide a common bully-proofing language to use throughout the school

▶ Convey a "no tolerance" approach to bullying

▶ Empower victims

▶ Motivate bullies to change

caring majority, but usually other students will raise concerns in the class discussion. A student needs to be consistently and dependably displaying the caring majority behaviors for the chance to be part of the caring majority community. The goal of this model is to have every student in the class be identified as part of the caring community. When skillfully managed, this model can provide powerful motivation for students to develop caring behaviors.

The one possible drawback of using this model is the perception of exclusion by students.

Keep in mind that students are encouraged toward the goal of creating a "safe, respectful, inclusive environment so teachers can teach and students can learn." If a student does not wish to be in the caring majority, that is fine as long as he or she agrees not to disrupt the previously stated goal. Once the caring majority is developed, teachers can use this group to solve behavioral problems by asking how they want to resolve a fight at recess or by having a caring majority student mentor another student who is having difficulties. The goal, regardless of the model adopted, is to develop an inclusionary model. Reinforce positive student behavior. Random reinforcers, rather than competitive ones, are preferred.

Collateral School-Wide Activities

In addition to the classroom caring majority reinforcement programs, collateral school-wide activities will help to spread the caring majority into a caring community. The following are some suggestions (a special thanks to Dr. Larry Epstein for sharing many of these ideas) for developing school-wide acknowledgments, celebrations, and rituals:

1. Use a school bulletin board to put pictures of every student in each classroom who belongs to the caring majority.

2. Create classroom special projects that are coordinated to reinforce the caring

majority concept throughout the school. For instance:

- caring majority posters in art

- research projects on historical figures who represent caring values

- putting books about caring on display in the library

- a musical production around these themes (selecting children to perform based on being in the caring majority, not by musical, acting, or dance talents)

3. Have a school-wide "sit with someone new at lunch day."

Guiding Principle Four

Using Teachable Moments

Use the opportunities students give through their day-to-day interactions. They will make mistakes. Every time a behavior is displayed that does not reinforce the goal of "a safe, respectful, inclusive environment so teachers can teach and students can learn," talk about the behavior. Most importantly, teach the right behavior. Turn opportunities into teachable moments.

By engaging in activities such as those suggested in the previous principles, a caring school environment is built. The goal is for this to carry over into the entire community so that each and every child at the school feels respected, cared for, and special.*

*The authors give profound thanks and appreciation to Vicky Temple, Psy.D., and Paul Von Essen, M.S.W., who creatively implemented these caring majority ideas and made them a part of many school communities.

Strategies of Intervention

LEVELS OF RISK

STRATEGIES OF INTERVENTION	LOW ⟵		⟶ HIGH
Not Joining In	Walk away.	Stay but do not participate.	Declare your non-participation.
Getting Adult Help	Get help anonymously.	Identify who the helpful adults are and get one of them.	Announce loudly your intention to get adult help; then do it.
Mobilizing Peer Group	Identify a peer leader and offer to join in standing up to the bully.	Identify others who are capable of mobilizing peers in defense of the victim and recruit them to the cause.	Be a leader in recruiting others to join in standing up to the bully.
Taking an Individual Stand	Go over to the victim and lead him or her away from the situation.	Say, "Leave him alone."	Say, "We don't treat people like that at our school."
Befriending the Victim	Privately empathize with the victim by saying, "That was unfair or cruel."	Go over and stand with the victim or invite him or her to join you in doing something else.	Stand with the victim and publicly announce the "unfair" behavior of the bully.

Copyright 2000 by Garrity, Baris, and Porter.

Caring Majority Recognition Form

_____
(Date)

Today, I observed _____ engaging in the following caring behavior:
(Name)

_____ Sticking up for a child who was being treated unkind

_____ Including a child who had been left out

_____ Stopping the spread of a rumor

_____ Getting adult assistance for a serious bully situation

_____ Displaying empathy

_____ Supporting diversity

_____ Other: _____

Your child typifies the kind of student we value at _____
(Name of School)

His/her behavior indicates that he/she has gone above and beyond the call of duty in demonstrating caring for others. His/her name will go on our Caring Majority Board and will be announced at the end of this week. Please take a few minutes to discuss this admirable behavior with your child.

_____   _____
Teacher Signature   Principal Signature

Developed by Larry Epstein and Lana Hansen

Certificate of Appreciation

Chapter Five
Collaboration With Parents

Working effectively with the community of parents is an important and integral component of a successful bully-proofing program. The development of a clear message from the school to the parents regarding bullying is a fundamental first step. A strong, clear position that bullying behavior will not be tolerated must be communicated to parents in order to build collaborative relationships between the school and home.

In the staff training component of this program (Chapter Four, Session 6) a plan for working with parents should have been developed. This plan should specify: (1) how parents will be informed about the classroom curriculum and kept apprised of developments with the bully-proofing program (suggestions include community meetings, newsletters/fliers, PTA involvement, telephone calls/meetings with staff members), (2) how parents should inform the school staff of a situation in which their child is being bullied, and (3) how parents will be informed when their child is bullying.

Many parents may have attended the orientation presentation to introduce the adoption of the *Bully-Proofing Your School* program, and all the parents will have received a letter inviting their participation in that presentation which briefly explained the program. Beyond those initial communications to parents, the ongoing message should not only specify behaviors that will not be tolerated, but should also educate parents about bullying and victim behaviors and strategies for handling each. The philosophy to be communicated should be one of working together to create a safe school environment with children exhibiting appropriate behaviors.

The parents should also be informed, with specific details, about the classroom curriculum. Strong assurances must be given to the parents that none of their children will be individually identified or labeled as either victim or bully.

Parents appreciate being informed of who at the school they can contact if they are concerned that their children are experiencing bullying. The staff training plan should specify a contact person for both parents of victims and parents of bullies. This person might be the classroom teacher or someone else, such as the facilitator, an administrator, or a member of the school's mental health team.

Overall, it is critical that the school take a position that no one benefits when harassment and destructive conflict are allowed to take place. Parents of bullies need to hear the same message that their children are hearing: "Bullying behavior is not allowed."

Periodic updates are encouraged in which parents are kept informed about the progress being made with the program as well as educated about teaching their children appropriate skills for avoiding and

defending against bullying behavior, both physical and verbal. Parents can help their children to become stronger and less vulnerable to attacks from other children, especially if they feel the support of the school staff toward providing a safe environment that allows learning to take place.

There are two "Golden Rules" to keep in mind when meeting with parents:

▶ **Most parents feel that their child is the victim.**
Even when bullying behavior has been documented, the majority of parents will argue that the victim was provocative and therefore caused the difficulty to arise.

▶ **It is essential to meet with concerned parents individually.**
Avoid, at all costs, bringing both the parent(s) of a bully and the parent(s) of a victim involved in a conflict together. If you do so, the conflict is likely to escalate with each set of parents defending their child and no solution reached. The parents of bullies and the parents of victims are dealing with entirely different problems; both need your assistance, but in very unique ways.

Specific guidelines for working collaboratively with both the parent(s) of a bully and the parent(s) of a victim are presented in the following two sections of this chapter.

The Parent(s) of a Bully

Parents and the school staff must work together to ensure that the school is a safe and caring environment. If a school staff truly believes that a certain child is a bully, it is not only their responsibility to stop the bullying and to protect the victim(s) but to inform the parent(s) of the bully.

First of all, decide who the right person in the school is to approach the parent(s) of the bully. It may not necessarily be the child's classroom teacher or the principal

or other administrator. It might be the facilitator of this program, the school counselor, or the student's former teacher who established rapport with the parent(s) the previous year. The best person is the one the parent(s) are the most likely to have respect for, to trust, and to feel is on their side rather than against them. It is also important not to "gang up" on the parent(s) by approaching them with multiple members of the school staff.

You should expect that the first reaction the parent(s) of a bully are likely to have when contacted is one of anger and defensiveness. They frequently feel that their child was provoked and that the bullying behavior was justified by the provocation. **Do not argue with this understanding of the problem.** A far more effective approach is to **remind them of the school's goal of creating a safe and caring environment** for all and that **solving problems with aggression is not a good solution regardless of the justification.** Let them know in no uncertain terms what the school's policy is regarding bullying and what the consequences of bullying behavior will be for their child.

There are three main points to remember when dealing with the bully as well as with the bully's parent(s):

1. Take a no-nonsense approach—bullying will not be an acceptable behavior within the school.

2. Set clear expectations for behavior and consequences for bullying behavior.

3. Have as little dialogue and discussion about the bullying behavior (i.e., excuses, justification) as possible.

While a no-nonsense stance should be taken with bullying behavior, it is critical that the parent(s) of the bully leave an initial meeting regarding their child with a sense of collaboration and rapport with the school staff. Emphasize the concept of assisting their child to learn how to have power without using aggression or bullying. Explain the idea of practicing and rehearsing appropriate behaviors as a more

RESOURCE GUIDE

See "Books for Parents" for sources of information on intervention and discipline for parents. Additionally, the books *Bully-Proofing Your Child: A Parent's Guide* and *Bully-Proofing Your Child: First Aid for Hurt Feelings* (Garrity, Baris, and Porter, 2000) may be suggested to parents.

effective learning tool than punishing the incorrect behaviors. Finally, establish together some behavioral lesson plans for home so that their child will be reinforced in both the home and school environment for appropriate and caring behaviors. Parents of bullies often need guidance in responding to their children empathetically while still setting limits and reinforcing appropriate behaviors (provide them with *Handout 39* and maybe *Handout 40* as a first step).

There are three important skills to encourage the parent(s) to practice:

1. Trying to identify their child's feeling, need, or motivation when an inappropriate behavior occurs (e.g., "You just said something very cruel to your brother. I wonder if you were feeling jealous that he got new shoes and you didn't?").

2. Setting a limit on the behavior (e.g., "It is **not** O.K. in our family to make someone else feel bad when you feel jealous.").

3. Teaching alternative behaviors that are acceptable ways to express the feeling (e.g., "It **is** O.K. for you to say that you don't like feeling left out and to ask us for some new shoes for yourself," or "It **is** O.K. to tell your brother that it hurts your feelings when he brags and carries on about his new shoes and to stop it," or "It **is** O.K. to tell your brother that you feel jealous and want something for yourself and would he let you play with something of his to help you feel better.").

The Parent(s) of a Victim

The school may not have to reach out to the parent(s) of the victimized child. Instead, the school staff is likely to find the parent(s) contacting them, angry and upset that their child has not received protection from bullying within the school. In these conversations, emotions often run high,

preventing calm dialogue and the feeling of mutuality between the parent(s) and the school.

Before these types of contacts occur, it is far better to let the community of parents know about the school's policy regarding bullying and to offer parents guidelines about who to approach and when to approach the school. **It is healthy and normal for parents to be advocates for their child.** While the school may traditionally tend to view these vocal parents as overprotective, it is important to remember that **children who are victimized usually do not have the skills to stop the bullying on their own. They need an advocate, and their parents are going to fill that role if the school staff does not.** Consequently, it is critical that the school set a tone (and communicate it to parents) of caring and protection; only then can the parents step aside and feel comfortable that the problem will be handled within the school.

While active concern on the part of the parents is quite common with children who are victimized, occasionally parents may not recognize the symptoms of victimization in their own child. The following characteristics assist in identifying victims, and can be communicated to the parent(s) if any apply to their child:

▶ A child who misses a great deal of school or makes multiple trips to the nurse's office may be attempting to avoid a bullying situation.

▶ A child who avoids the cafeteria or playground may be attempting to avoid a bullying situation.

▶ Sometimes a drop in a child's academic performance thought to be due to a learning problem is actually the result of bullying.

▶ A shy child, a child who stands on the sidelines during activity time, a child who appears isolated and/or depressed during school, is the type of child most likely to be picked on and bullied.

Children who are victimized are not likely to tell an adult themselves; the school staff must take responsibility for identifying these children and letting them know that someone cares and will keep them safe. Part of that process is contacting the victim's parent(s). Talking with the parent(s) and listening to their input can be very revealing. Often information is shared that helps the school staff to understand the reasons why that individual child is being bullied.

In particular, the parents of victims should be asked about the three most common triggers of victimization by peers:

▶ **Inhibition and shyness that is temperamentally based.**
Some children are naturally shy and have been that way their entire lives. These children are inhibited in general about approaching others or being evaluated by others. These children lack the necessary social skills for effective peer interaction (and benefit greatly from coaching). They are also likely to have overprotective parents who have naturally looked out for them during much of their lives because of their inherent shyness.

▶ **Trauma or loss of a significant magnitude, resulting in anxiety and fear surrounding peer interaction.**
These are children who have been hurt in life; they are afraid and anxious much of the time. They protect themselves by withdrawing; they are overly sensitive and easily hurt. Small amounts of teasing can retrigger earlier trauma and result in further withdrawal which, sadly, often has as a consequence increased bullying and rejection by peers.

Children with significant learning disabilities, physical disabilities, and/or social processing difficulties can also be classified in this group. These children are not inherently shy, but their past history or unique circumstances cause high anxiety and fearfulness.

▶ **Physical weakness or petite size, especially in boys.**
Boys who are physically weak or small are extremely prone to victimization. Family dynamics surrounding these characteristics can often become significant factors as well. Boys who are physically weak, for instance, are more at risk to be rejected by their fathers who often are critical and distant toward them. Mothers, on the other hand, tend to protect their sons when they are not of strong stature.

All three of these categories of children require protection within the school environment. While addressing the family dynamics or individual personality characteristics can help, that alone will not stop victimization without strong support and caring from the staff within the school.

Working together as caring adults in the lives of these children is the kindest and most effective approach to preventing victimization. The child who is traumatized may also benefit from individual or supportive group psychotherapy. Children who are learning disabled and physically disabled may be helped by a strongly supportive home environment as well as an educative approach to their peers at school designed to build compassion and understanding of their disability. Finally, the child who is physically weak can occasionally be assisted by skill and strength development such as a karate or judo class. Some children will resist these types of assistance and these students' special contributions, be it a musical talent, hobby, or unusual interest, must be identified and capitalized on within the school setting.

The parents of children who are victimized are frequently overinvolved and overly protective of their children. These parents are usually compassionate and quick to identify with their children's emotional pain. Rather than criticizing their protective stance, it will be most helpful for the school to assist the parents in gradually restructuring and reshaping their ways of offering protection to their children. Simply asking concerned parents to trust that the school will keep their children safe is unlikely to be successful. In reality, their children have not been kept safe within the school and the parents have no reason to trust that they will be in the future without specific responses from the school staff that help them establish such trust.

Parents of children who are victimized will need frequent communications, in person or in writing, as to how playground time or lunchtime (two times when children are most vulnerable to bullying) went for their child. A "behavioral journal" that is sent home each Friday can be a helpful tool. The child who is victimized might have an identified social skill to practice each week within both the home and the school environment. A daily log could be kept within the journal of the number of times the child was observed displaying the identified skill. The parent(s) will value and appreciate these written remarks. And while this procedure may be time consuming initially, it will frequently offer the parent(s) of the child who is victimized the reassurance they need that someone is looking out for their child and that the parent(s) and the school are a team working together for the growth and well-being of the child.

Handout 37 provides some specific strategies to prevent and cope with bullying behavior that parents of children who are victimized can review with and reinforce in their children. It is helpful to provide this handout to parent(s) at the initial meeting for their future reference, explaining that these skills will be taught to their child within the school as well. *Handout 38* can also be provided at this time.

What Parents Can Do . . .

How to Find Out if Your Child Is Being Bullied

What to look for:
- Excuses for not wanting to go to school
- Unexplained bruises
- Torn clothing

- Need for extra school supplies or money
- Continually "loses" belongings and school supplies
- Problems sleeping/nightmares
- Sudden loss of appetite
- Sudden academic problems
- Secretive/sullen/temper outbursts
- Ravenous after school—Ask Why: someone may be taking lunch or money
- Rushes to bathroom after school—Ask Why: your child may be frightened to use bathroom at school due to threats
- School reports frequent visits to the nurse with mysterious complaints, especially after recess (may be to avoid or need for nurturance)

If You Suspect a Problem
- Make it a habit to talk to your child about school.
- Ask pointed questions such as "Who is a bully in your class?" "Who bothers kids at recess and on the bus?"

Tips for Parents of Victims to Give Their Children

1. Don't react emotionally.

Assist your child in knowing who the safe people are within the school to go to when bullied. Help them practice not showing strong emotions in front of the bully. This only excites the bully more. Instead, tell them to quickly go to someone identified as safe.

2. Be assertive.

This works best if the bully is alone and not with a group of other children who will give him or her strength. If assertiveness is appropriate, tell your child to simply state that he or she does not like the bullying behavior, that it is not allowed, and that he or she intends to tell someone if it does not stop.

3. Stay with others.

Reinforce for your child that bullies are most likely to act aggressively with a child who is alone.

4. Do something unexpected.

This is especially effective if the child can turn the bullying situation into something humorous. Encourage your child's sense of humor and creative problem-solving skills.

5. Own the put-down.

Remind your child that a bully often does not know what to do or say next if the victim simply agrees with him or her.

How to Help: Steps to Bully-Proof Your Child

1. Let the school know your safety worries immediately.

2. Keep a record of time, date, names, and circumstances to show a pattern of harassment.

3. Urge your school to adopt a clear conduct code that enforces strict penalties for students who break the rules against bullying.

4. Teach your child self-respect—confident kids are less likely to become a victim.

5. Let your child know it is O.K. to express anger if done appropriately.

6. Encourage friendships—there is strength in numbers.

7. Arrange weekend play dates to promote friendships.

8. Build social skills early.

9. Help shy kids with social skills training—role play together situations that have occurred previously.

10. Explain the difference between telling and tattling. Tattling is when you report something just to get someone in trouble. Telling is when you report that you or someone else is in danger. (Verbal abuse and being excluded are dangers too.)

11. Stress the importance of body language—a "victim stance" may attract bullies.

12. Teach your child effective skills for making friends such as how to share, compromise, apologize, use "I" statements, change the topic to avoid conflict, and use a "diplomatic" approach.

13. Teach your child alternative responses—**HA HA, SO**
    (**H**elp, **A**void, **H**umor, **A**ssert Yourself, **S**elf-Talk, **O**wn It).

14. Don't advise either ignoring or physically attacking the bully.

What to Do if You Find Out Your Child Bullies Other Youngsters

▶ Evaluate whether the behavior might be modeled from parents. If not, is bullying of a younger sibling tolerated? Family therapy may be needed if patterns are difficult to change.

▶ Do not use physical punishment for discipline; that encourages a child to humiliate and hurt others. Instead, remove privileges or add jobs around the house.

▶ Provide as much parental (or substitute parental) supervision as possible.

▶ Put an immediate stop to any bullying you observe. Always have the child act in a more appropriate way.

▶ Emphasize praise and positive feedback. Reward the child for caring and appropriate behaviors.

Bullying Behaviors Chart

	Mild		Moderate		Severe	
Physical Agression:						
▶ Pushing	▶ Kicking	▶ Defacing property	▶ Physical acts that are demeaning and humiliating, but not bodily harmful (e.g., de-panting)	▶ Physical violence against family or friends	▶ Threatening with a weapon	
▶ Shoving	▶ Hitting	▶ Stealing			▶ Inflicting bodily harm	
▶ Spitting			▶ Locking in a closed or confined space			
Social Alienation:						
▶ Gossiping	▶ Setting up to look foolish	▶ Ethnic slurs	▶ Publicly humiliating (e.g., revealing personal information)	▶ Maliciously excluding	▶ Threatening with total isolation by peer group	
▶ Embarrassing	▶ Spreading rumors about	▶ Setting up to take the blame	▶ Excluding from group	▶ Manipulating social order to achieve rejection		
			▶ Social rejection	▶ Malicious rumor-mongering		
Verbal Aggression:						
▶ Mocking	▶ Teasing about clothing or possessions	▶ Teasing about appearance	▶ Intimidating telephone calls	▶ Verbal threats of aggression against property or possessions	▶ Verbal threats of violence or of inflicting bodily harm	
▶ Name calling						
▶ Dirty looks						
▶ Taunting						
Intimidation:						
▶ Threatening to reveal personal information	▶ Defacing property or clothing	▶ Taking possessions (e.g., lunch, clothing, toys)	▶ Extortion	▶ Threats of using coercion against family or friends	▶ Coercion	
▶ Graffiti	▶ Playing a dirty trick		▶ Sexual/racial taunting		▶ Threatening with a weapon	
▶ Publicly challenging to do something						

Copyright 1992 Garrity and Baris.

Conclusion

Parents feel concern these days. They have every right to. Knowing their children's school has adopted the *Bully-Proofing Your School* program relieves some of their fear and anxiety. It conveys a message of care and concern as well as an awareness that bully-victim problems are real.

Years ago too many schools ignored this issue and those that adopted such a program worried that parents would jump to the conclusion that they alone had bully problems. Today, most parents recognize bully-victim problems as something that every school experiences. Rather than judging a school with a program as an unsafe environment, they feel grateful that the problem is acknowledged and addressed. Most parents are eager for information.

No child in any school is immune from this problem today. Each plays a unique role; some are victims, some are bullies, the rest are either part of the silent majority or the caring majority. The parents of each play a part in your school community. The parents of a victim will benefit their child by reinforcing the classroom lessons through other teachable moments in their home. The parents of silent majority children often benefit from knowing how to distinguish normal peer conflict from true bullying. The parents of bullies need to know early on about their child's unhealthy power tactics. If they are defensive or unable to acknowledge the problem, they still need to know the school's policy and disciplinary plan.

Bibliography

Binswanger-Friedman, L., & Ciner, A. (1991, November). Unpublished material presented to Graland School, Denver, CO.

Eron, L. (1987). Aggression through the ages. *School Safety,* Fall, 12–16.

Federal Bureau of Investigations. (2001). *The school shooter: A perspective on risk factors.* Washington, D.C.: F.B.I.

Garrity, C., Boris, M., and Porter, W. (2000). *Bully-Proofing Your Child: A parents' guide.* Longmont, CO: Sopris West.

Goldstein, A., & Glick, B. (1987). *Aggression replacement training.* Champaign, IL: Research Press.

Goleman, D. (1995). *Emotional intelligence.* New York: Bantam Books.

Gottman, J. (1997). *Raising an emotionally intelligent child.* New York: Simon and Schuster.

Greenbaum, S., Turner, B., & Stephens, R. (1989). *Set straight on bullies.* Malibu, CA: Pepperdine University Press.

Hodson, J. (1992). Bullying in schools: Mainstream and special needs. *Support for Learning,* 7(1), 3–7.

Huggins, P. (1994). *Building self-esteem in the classroom: Intermediate version.* Longmont, CO: Sopris West.

Huggins, P. (1993). *Teaching friendship skills: Intermediate version.* Longmont, CO: Sopris West.

Huggins, P. (1993). *Teaching friendship skills: Primary version.* Longmont, CO: Sopris West.

Kreidler, W.J. (1984). *Creative conflict resolution.* Glenview, IL: Scott Foresman.

Lee, F. (1993, April 4). Disrespect rules. The New York Times Educational Supplement, p. 16.

Lewis, D.O. (1992). From abuse to violence: Psychophysiological consequences of maltreatment. *Journal of the American Academy of Child and Adolescent Psychiatry,* 31, 383–391.

Olweus, D. (1978). *Aggression in the schools: Bullies and whipping boys.* Washington, D.C.: Hemisphere (Wiley).

Olweus, D. (1991). Bully/victim problems among school children: Basic facts and effects of a school based intervention program. In D. Pepler & K. Rubin (Eds.), *The development and treatment of childhood aggression.* Hillsdale, NJ: Lawrence Erlbaum.

Olweus, D. (1993). *Bullying at school: What we know and what we can do.* Cambridge, MA: Blackwell.

Paley, V.G. (1992). *You can't say, you can't play.* Cambridge, MA: Howard University Press.

Pepler, D., & Craig, W. (1995a). A peek behind the fence: Naturalistic observations of aggressive children with remote audiovisual recording. *Developmental Psychology,* 31(4), 548–553.

Pepler, D., & Craig, W. (1995b). Peer processes in bullying and victimization: An observational study. *Exceptional Education Canada,* 5(3–4), 81–95.

Pepler, D.J., Craig, W., & Roberts, W. (1998). Observations of aggressive and nonaggressive children on the school playground. *Merrill-Palmer Quarterly,* 44, 55-76.

Perry, D., Willard, J., & Perry, L. (1990). Peers' perception of the consequences that victimized children provide aggressors. *Child Development,* 61, 1289-1309.

Prelutsky, J. (1984). *The new kid on the block.* New York: Scholastic.

Samenow, S. (1984). *Inside the criminal*

mind. New York: Random House.

Samenow, S. (1989). *Before it's too late: Why some kids get into trouble and what parents can do about it.* New York: Random House.

Schwartz, D. (2000). Subtypes of victims and aggressors in children's peer groups. *Journal of Abnormal Child Psychology, 28,* 181-192.

Shure, M., & Spirack, G. (1978). *Problem solving techniques in childrearing.* San Francisco, CA: Jossey Bass.

Spirack, G., Platt, J., & Shure, M. (1976). *The problem solving approach to adjustment.* San Francisco, CA: Jossey Bass.

Stephenson, P., & Smith, D. (1989). Bullying in two English comprehensive schools. In E. Roland and E. Munthe (Eds.), *Bullying: An international perspective.* London: Fulton.

Resource Guide

This Resource Guide is divided into six major sections: (1) Videotapes and Films for Educators and Parents, (2) Videotapes and Films for Students, (3) Books for Educators, (4) Books for Parents, (5) Books for Primary Students, and (6) Books for Intermediate Students. The videotapes and films to be used for students are identified for use with early or late elementary levels within their descriptions. Most entries are annotated so that you can select resources according to your specific needs. For example, if your class is working on Lesson 3 of the classroom curriculum, you would want to select stories that build empathy for the victim. Lessons 5 and 6, on the other hand, offer strategies for the caring majority to support the victims and books incorporating this type of content material would be best used for these sessions.

It is important that you select the films, videotapes, and stories shared with the students with care. Some of the materials designated for the later elementary aged students could traumatize a first or second grader. Similarly, some of the content depicted in certain videos is graphic and upsetting both to young children as well as to children who may have experienced a similar bullying situation in their own lives. If content of any of the Resource Guide entries is particularly explicit, a "caution" is provided. It is recommended that you first view or read anything with a caution prior to sharing it with either the students or the staff.

Videotapes and Films for Educators and Parents

Bus Discipline. (1992). Distributed by Sopris West, 4093 Specialty Place, Longmont, CO 80504.

A four-tape set that presents informa-

tion on setting policies that are positive, trains drivers in management, shows teachers how to support safe policies, and gives a step-by-step process for solving behavior problems.

Cafeteria Discipline. (1995). Distributed by Sopris West, 4093 Specialty Place, Longmont, CO 80504.

Foundations: Establishing Positive Discipline Policies. (1992). Sopris West, 4093 Specialty Place, Longmont, CO 80504.

Helps school staff design policies and procedures that create a solid base of positive behavior management techniques. Includes three text volumes and six videotape sessions.

How I Learned Not To Be Bullied. (1997). Sunburst, 101 Castleton St. Pleasantville, NY 10570. 1-800-431-1934.

Easy-to-learn strategies for elementary-aged children to use when bullied.

Managing Acting-Out Behavior: A Staff Development Program. (1992). Distributed by Sopris West, 4093 Specialty Place, Longmont, CO 80504.

A two-video set that teaches teachers, school administrators, and service providers how to cope successfully with explosive behavior, physical aggression, verbal abuse, severe tantrums, open defiance, and insubordination.

Michael's Story: The No Blame Approach. (1990). Lame Duck Publishing, 71 South Road, Portshead, Bristol BS20 90Y.

Produced in England, this video introduces a step-by-step, teacher-led program that has been successful in the English schools for helping victims and stopping perpetrators of bullying behavior.

Playground Discipline. (1991). Distributed by Sopris West, 4093 Specialty Place, Longmont, CO 80504.

A two-video set that trains teaching and playground staff in setting up a safe playground environment and designing consistent and effective expectations and clear procedures. Specific playground scenes very effectively show how to interact with students, deal with crises, implement consequences, and deal with fighting. A very helpful video for training playground aides.

Set Straight on Bullies. (1988). National School Safety Center, 4165 Thousand Oaks Boulevard, Suite 290, Westlake Village, CA 91362.

An 18-minute video that presents the story of a young boy victimized by a bully. The video is designed to educate school staff and students that bullying is a problem that adversely effects everyone within a school environment if it is tolerated.

Stamp Out Bullying. (1990). Lame Duck Publishing, 71 South Road, Portshead, Bristol BS20 90Y.

Produced in England, this video illustrates a training workshop in an English school that was the result of a 14-year-old girl's suicide attempt following a bullying incident.

Videotapes and Films for Students

Broken Toy. (1992). Summerhill Productions, 846 1/2 McIntire Avenue, Zanesville, OH 43701.

A 25-minute video that depicts a number of realistic scenarios in the life of a 12-year-old boy who is ridiculed and physically assaulted at school. Not only is the home life of the victim portrayed, but the main bully's family is also depicted. While the story builds empathy for the victim, the content is dra-

matic. The ending, however, restores hope. The goal of this video is to build awareness and compassion in the bullies by showing them how much emotional damage their behavior can cause. For grades 5 and up. Preview before using.

Bullyproof (1997). Future Wave, Inc., 105 Camino Teresa, Santa Fe, NM 87505. (505) 982-882; fax: (505) 982-6460.

For younger children, a puppet show program is available that includes a portable stage, sound-track tape, curriculum, and supplies for creating a performance. For older children and teens, a rap and roll opera is available on video.

". . . but names will never hurt me" (1997). Kids Hope, 206 Bascomb Springs Court, Woodstock, GA 30189-3550. 1-800-465-4758.

A video-based program for grades 1–6 that helps children discover the value of treating others with kindness and respect. A step-by-step study guide is included. It is a powerful story about an overweight girl who struggles with acceptance until one individual stands up for her and sets an important example of Caring Community behavior.

In Harm's Way. (1996). Agency for Instructional Technology, Box A, Bloomington, IN 47402-0120. (800) 457-4509.

A 15-minute video to help students deal with bullies or name calling. Program also includes teacher's guide, song book, audio cassette with 17 songs. Recommended for grades 3–5.

The Choice. (1981). Phoenix/BFA Films, 2349 Chaffee Drive, St. Louis, MO 63146. (314) 569-0211; (800) 221-1274.

Available as a video or filmstrip, this is the story of how three boys struggle with their relationship when a new boy attempts to enter their group. The film is a good example of bully-victim relationships and of how the caring majority can be helpful.

Coping With Bullying. (1991). James Slanfield Company, Drawer G, P.O. Box 41058, Santa Barbara, CA 93140.

A three-video set with a teacher's guide to help students understand and recognize bullying behavior. Various assertive responses are demonstrated as ways to respond to bullying. Recommended for grades 6 and up.

Hopscotch—Revised. (1987). SVE and Churchill, 6677 North Northwest Highway, Chicago, IL 60631-1304. (800) 829-1900.

This video is the animated story of a boy who wants to make friends and tries showing off his prowess, parading his possessions, being noisy and disruptive, acting tough, and flattering other children. Finally, he stops playing roles and is accepted. Recommended for grades K–6.

Standing Up For Yourself. (1986). Phoenix/BFA Films, 2349 Chaffee Drive, St. Louis, MO 63146. (314) 569-0211 or 1-800-221-1274.

Part of the Taking Responsibility series of tapes, this video reminds the viewer that some attempts to be assertive will not be successful and that sometimes it is necessary to get help from adults. This tape is excellent reinforcement of the HA HA SO strategies. Recommended for grades K–6.

Books for Educators

Asher, S. & Gottman, J. (Eds.). (1981). *The development of children's friendships.* Cambridge, MA: Cambridge University Press.

Beland, K. *Second step.* Committee for Children, 2203 Airport Way South, Ste. 500, Seattle, WA 98134. 1-800-634-4449.

A curriculum guide for teaching empathy problem solving and anger management from preschool through eighth grade.

Blanco, J. (2003). *Please stop laughing at me: One woman's inspirational story.* Avon, MA: Adams Media.

Borba, M. (1989). *Esteem builders.* Rolling Hills Estates, CA: Jalmar Press.

This self-esteem curriculum is designed for grades K–8, and presents specific ideas for improving student achievement and behavior as well as the overall school climate.

Borba, M. & Borba, C. (1978). *Self-esteem: A classroom affair.* Oak Grove, MN: Winston Press.

Center for Applied Psychology. (1993). *Face your feelings! A book to help children learn about feelings.* King of Prussia, PA: Author.

Chicola, N.A. & English, E.B. (2002). *Creating caring communities with books kids love.* Golden, CO: Fulcrum Publishing.

Specifically targeted for grades K through 6, this book (which is organized by 6 levels of community: Personal, family, school, neighborhood, nation, and world) encourages a collective "caring" identity among children using a variety of instructional strategies and engaging activities through the integration of fiction and nonfiction children's literature.

Diamond, J.A. (1996). *Friendship note paper.* Denver, CO: Great Eye-deas Press.

This book describes a curriculum project appropriate from kindergarten through the elementary years. The project is multifaceted and the children successfully learn many skills including what a friend is, how to be a good friend, how to work together on a project, and how to carry that project to the community in the form of a fundraiser.

CAUTION

Drew, N. (1987). *Learning the skills of peacemaking.* Rolling Hills Estates, CA: Jalmar Press.

This creative activity guide for elementary-aged children assists them in learning self-awareness, understanding of others, and mediation skills.

Goldstein, A. & Glick, B. (1987). *Aggression replacement training.* Champaign, IL: Research Press.

Presents a ten-week-long training session for teachers or mental health staff to use for anger control with adolescents, specifically, but could be adapted for elementary-aged students. A guide to moral training is also included.

Greenbaum, S., Turner, B., & Stephens, R. (1989). *Set straight on bullies.* Malibu, CA: Pepperdine University, National School Safety Foundation.

Presents statistics on bullying in the schools as well as guidelines for recognition of bullies and victims. Prevention strategies for changing the attitudes and actions of adults and students alike are provided.

Hoover, J.H. & Oliver, R. (1996). *The bullying prevention handbook: A guide for principals, teachers, and counselors.* Bloomington, IN: National Education Service.

This book is a wonderful resource for addressing bully-victim problems during the preadolescent and adolescent years. Sound research is provided that documents the middle school years as the worst in terms of the intensity of bullying experienced. A comprehensive approach that promotes prevention through education.

Huggins, P. (1990). *Teaching cooperation skills.* Longmont, CO: Sopris West.

Includes a series of lessons and experiential activities designed to teach both primary and intermediate students the skills necessary for cooperative learning to take place. Lessons focus on the skills of self-management, listening, collaborative problem solving, and leadership. Students learn to resolve conflicts through negotiation and compromise.

Huggins, P. (1991). *Creating a caring classroom.* Longmont, CO: Sopris West.

A collection of strategies designed to promote mutual support and strength connections in the classroom. Included are: (1) getting-acquainted activities, (2) classroom management procedures, (3) a personal/social behavior scale and behavior improvement strategies for students with special needs, (4) a relaxation training program, and (5) a large collection of activities for establishing a nurturing classroom community. Designed for use with both primary and intermediate students.

Huggins, P. (1993). *Helping kids handle anger* (2nd ed.). Longmont, CO: Sopris West.

Includes lessons designed to enable both primary and intermediate students to acknowledge, accept, and constructively express anger. Students learn: (1) to use inner speech to inhibit aggressive behavior, (2) to use thinking skills to choose constructive behavior when angry, (3) appropriate language to express anger, (4) a variety of techniques to release energy after anger arousal, (5) ways to defuse the anger of others, and (6) a model for resolving classroom conflicts. Role plays and puppets are utilized to encourage active student involvement.

Huggins, P. (1993). *Teaching friendship skills* (Primary and Intermediate versions). Longmont, CO: Sopris West.

This version contains all new lessons and supplementary activities. Students identify behaviors in others that attract them and behaviors that alienate them. They examine their own behavior and determine changes they need to make in order to gain friends. They learn how to curb physical and verbal aggression.

They discover that the secret to making friends is to make others feel special and practice specific ways to do so. They learn the value of sharing and how to give sincere compliments and apologies.

Huggins, P. (1994). *Building self-esteem in the classroom* (Primary and Intermediate versions). Longmont, CO: Sopris West.

This version contains all new lessons and activities. Students refine their self-descriptions and acquire an appreciation for their uniqueness. They are introduced to the concept of multiple intelligences and learn a process by which they can determine their own strong intelligences. They learn the cognitive skill of self-encouragement, which enables them to respond to mistakes, failures, or put-downs in a manner that maintains their self-esteem. They learn to take responsibility for their school success by using self-statements to motivate and coach themselves through academic tasks.

Huggins, P. (1994). *Helping kids find their strengths*. Longmont, CO: Sopris West.

Designed to enable students to identify and utilize their strengths. Based on pioneering research by Bernard Haldane, Ph.D., and the Dependable Strengths Project Team at the University of Washington. Students build self-esteem not by positive thinking, but by analyzing experiences they're proud of for clues regarding their core strengths. Students share their good experiences, then utilize teacher and peer input to "tease out" the strengths that helped them create those experiences. They learn a large strength vocabulary and use their expanded self-identity as a springboard for new successes. In helping others find their strengths, students develop a respect for diversity.

Huggins, P. (1998). *Helping kids handle put downs*. Longmont, CO: Sopris West.

Students learn the art of ignoring; surprising antagonizers by "agreeing" with them; disarming antagonizers with humor; and deflecting verbal aggression with "crazy compliments." These strategies win respect and de-escalate conflict. Students also learn to use self-encouragement to dispel the hurt of put-downs and maintain their self-respect. Includes lesson presentation instructions and reproducibles. Grades 1–6.

Huggins, P. (1999). *Helping kids handle conflict*. Longmont, CO: Sopris West.

Students come to understand that they possess the power to manage their anger and conflicts by using the simple Stop, Think, and Pick a Plan (STP) process. They master skills such as ignoring, using chance, stating what they want, and making a deal. STP techniques are then applied to real-life situations. Grades 1–3.

Iowa Peace Institute. (1992). *Fostering peace*. Grinnell, IA: Author.

A comparison of nine different conflict resolution approaches for use with both elementary and high school-aged students.

Jackson, N.F., Jackson, D.A., & Monroe, C. (1983). *Getting along with others: Teaching social effectiveness to children*. Champaign, IL: Research Press.

Includes a program guide and activities packet. The program covers 17 social skills and the steps required to teach them. Each lesson includes role plays, relaxation training, activities, and homework assignments.

Jenson, W.R., Rhode, G., & Reavis, H.K. (1994). *The tough kid tool box*. Longmont, CO: Sopris West.

A companion piece to *The Tough Kid Book*, provides teachers with straight-forward, classroom tested, ready-to-use (reproducible) materials for managing and motivating tough to teach students.

Kaufman, G. & Raphael, L. (1990). *Stick up for yourself: Teacher's guide*. Minneapolis, MN: Free Spirit Publishing.

A comprehensive guide to a ten-part course that correlates with the book by the same title. Blends self-esteem and assertiveness with activities for a full year in the classroom. Recommended for grades 4–8.

Kreidler, W. (1984). *Creative conflict resolution*. Glenview, IL: Scott Foresman.

Presents techniques for creating a caring classroom environment. Exercises for assessing the students' behavior as well as concrete activities for promoting cooperation are specifically presented. Grades K–6 are covered.

Lavigna, G.L. & Donnellan, A.M. (1986). *Alternatives to punishment: Solving behavior problems with nonaversive strategies*. New York: Irvington.

Lee, J. (1993). *Facing the fire: Experiencing and expressing anger appropriately*. New York: Bantam Books.

A guide to understanding and expressing anger. Demonstrates ways to constructively face anger and experience it without losing control or hurting yourself or someone you love.

Loescher, E. (1991). *Peacemaking made practical: A conflict management curriculum for the elementary school*. Denver, CO: The Conflict Center.

A practical curriculum with over 50 lesson plans in developing an awareness of the feelings of self and others, social skills, and problem solving. All of the content is designed for the elementary level student and many clever applications of conflict resolution are included for the K–3 classroom.

McGinnis, E. & Goldstein, A.P. (1984). *Skillstreaming the elementary school child*. Champaign, IL: Research Press.

The program covers 60 specific prosocial skills such as saying "thank you," asking for help, apologizing, dealing with anger, responding to teasing, and handling group pressure. Addresses the needs of students who display aggression, immaturity, withdrawal, and other problem behaviors.

Paley, V.G. (1992). *You can't say, you can't play*. Cambridge, MA: Harvard University Press.

Details an experimental year in the kindergarten classroom of Vivian Paley, an innovative teacher and educator, who introduces the rule "You can't say, 'You can't play.' " Not only are the voices of the children heard as they adapt to this new order, but those of the older fifth graders observing the process are shared as well.

Paley, V.G. (1999). *The kindness of children*. Cambridge, MA: Harvard University Press.

This book explores children's impulsive goodness. It contends that although each child comes into the world with an instinct for kindness, it is a lesson that must be reinforced at every turn. Paley showcases a collection of gems about children's spontaneous acts of goodness.

Peace Education Foundation, 1900 Biscayne Blvd., Miami, FL 33132-1025. (305) 576-5075.

An educational organization devoted to teaching children creative and nondestructive ways to handle conflicts. Curriculum guides, family support materials, and school-based training available.

Prutzman, P., Stern, L., Burger, M.L., & Bodenhamer, G. (1988). *The friendly classroom for a small planet*. Philadelphia, PA: New Society Publishers.

Presents techniques for nonviolence, cooperation, and problem solving for grades K–6 developed by the Reconciliation Quakers and used by more than 20,000 teachers and parents.

Rhode, G., Jenson, W.R., & Reavis, H.K. (1992). *The tough kid book: Practical classroom management strategies*. Longmont, CO: Sopris West.

A resource for both regular and special education teachers, providing research-validated solutions designed to maximally reduce disruptive behavior in tough kids without big investments on the teacher's part in terms of time, money, and emotion. The solutions also provide tough kids with behavioral, academic, and social survival skills. It contains a wealth of ready-to-use information and lists other commercially available, practical resources for teachers who want more.

Rubin, A. (1980). *Children's friendships*. Cambridge, MA: Harvard University Press.

A wonderful book that traces friendships developmentally from the preschool-aged child through adolescence.

Schmidt, F. & Friedman, A. (1985). *Creative conflict solving for kids grades 4–9*. Miami, FL: Peaceworks.

Activities for use with the upper elementary grades.

Shapiro, L. (1993). *The building blocks of self-esteem: Activity book*. King of Prussia, PA: Center for Applied Psychology.

Sprick, R.S. (1981). *The solution book: A guide to classroom discipline*. Chicago, IL: Science Research Associates. 1-800-468-5850.

STOP Violence Coalition, 9307 W. 74th St., Merriam, KS 66204. (913) 432-5158.

An organization devoted to preventing interpersonal violence through public awareness, education, and promotion of alternatives. Material available for all ages.

Teaching Tolerance Project. (1997). *Starting small: Teaching tolerance in preschool and the early grades*. Montgomery, AL: Southern Poverty Law Center.

Trovato, C. (1987). *Teaching kids to care*. Cleveland, OH: Instructor Books.

A guide to understanding and developing a prosocial environment both within the classroom as well as within the home. Specifically focuses on ages 2–6 with special chapters on disabilities and ethnic differences.

Walker, H.M. (1995). *The acting-out child* (2nd ed.). Longmont, CO: Sopris West.

Wilt, J. & Watson, B. (1978). *Relationship builders*. Waco, TX: Educational Products.

Books for Parents

Blanco, J. (2003). *Please stop laughing at me: One woman's inspirational story*. Avon, MA: Adams Media.

Blechman, E. (1985). *Solving child behavior problems at home and school*. Champaign, IL: Research Press.

Canter, L. & Canter, M. (1988). *Assertive discipline for parents*. Santa Monica, CA: Lee Canter and Associates.

Dosick, W. (1995). *Golden rules: The ten ethical values parents need to teach their children*. San Francisco, CA: Harper Collins.

Eyre, L. & Eyre, R. (1993). *Teaching your children values*. New York: Simon and Schuster.

Fleischman, M. (1983). *Troubled families: A treatment program*. Champaign, IL: Research Press.

Frankel, F. (1996). *Good friends are hard to find*. Los Angeles, CA: Perspective Publishing.

Specific steps for parents and children to follow together for handling problems in friendships.

Garber, S.W., Garber, M.D., & Spizman, R.F. (1990). *If your child is hyperactive, inattentive, impulsive, distractible: Helping the ADD/ hyperactive child*. New York: Villard Books.

Golant, M. & Crane, B. (1987). *Sometimes it's okay to be angry: A parent/child manual for the education of children.* Indianapolis, IN: OK Press.

Goleman, D. (1995). *Emotional intelligence.* New York: Bantam Books.

Greer, C. & Kohl, G. (1995). *A call to character.* New York: Harper Collins.

James, J. (1990). *You know I wouldn't say this if I didn't love you.* New York: Newmarket Press.

Chapter Seven of this book presents helpful information about the principles of verbal self-defense and effective come-back statements that parents can teach their children.

McCoy, Elin. (1997). *What to do when kids are mean to your child.* New York: The Reader's Digest Association.

Real solutions are presented from the experts', parents', and kids' point-of-view. The format is excellent and easy to use.

Samenow, S. (1989). *Before it's too late: Why some kids get into trouble and what parents can do about it.* New York: Random House.

This book describes the thinking patterns of antisocial children and shows parents how they might inadvertently be facilitating the antisocial behavior. Easy to read and understand, this book is full of good ideas for parents and professionals alike.

Schulman, M., & Mekler, E. (1994). *Bringing up a moral child: A new approach to teaching your child to be kind, just and responsible.* New York: Doubleday.

A variety of ideas for building empathy, fairness, and moral development in children from birth through adolescence.

Seligman, M. (1995). *The optimistic child.* New York: Harper Perennial.

Shure, M.B. (1994). *Raising a thinking child: Help your child learn to resolve conflicts and get along with others.* New York: Holt.

Thompson, M., & O'Neill Grace, C. (2001). *Best friends, worst enemies: Understanding the social lives of children.* New York: Ballantine Books.

Examines in easy to read and engaging text how children's firendships shape and change developmentally.

Trovato, C. (1987). *Teaching kids to care.* Cleveland, OH: Instructor Books.

A guide to understanding and developing a prosocial environment both within the classroom as well as within the home. Specifically focuses on ages 2–6 with special chapters on disabilities and ethnic differences.

Books for Primary Students

Agassi, M. (2000). *Hands are not for hitting.* MN: Free Spirit Publishing Inc.

This book teaches children positive and appropriate ways to handle strong feelings without hitting.

Alexander, M. (1981). *Move over, twerp.* New York: Dial Books.

An enchanting story showing the resourcefulness of a young boy who employs humor to solve a bullying problem. The victim is very endearing—a great caring majority book. Unfortunately, this book is out of print. Visit your library for a copy.

Bennett, W.J. (Ed.) (1995). *The children's book of virtues.* New York: Simon & Schuster.

Classic stories, verses, poems, and fables are organized around different themes, each of which teaches a value. Courage, compassion, and honesty are just a few of the character values the book covers. It is short, easy to read, and a wonderful way to impart values through the timeless tradition of reading and storytelling.

Berenstein, S. & Berenstein, J. (1982). *The Berenstein Bears get in a fight.* New York: Random House.

In this popular story, Brother Bear and Sister Bear learn that sometimes even people who love each other get in fights, and that these are normal occurrences.

Berenstein, S. & Berenstein, J. (1993). *The Berenstein Bears and the bully.* New York: Random House.

Sister Bear has trouble with a bully. Brother Bear tries to help her learn coping strategies. The story has a positive outcome.

Boyd, L. (1991). *Bailey the big bully.* New York: Puffin Books.

This story wins by persuasion, showing a bully that it is more fun to be a friend. Go to your library for this one— it is out of print.

Brown, L., & Brown, M. (1998). *How to be a friend: A guide to making friends and keeping them.* Boston, MA: Little, Brown, & Co.

This guide explores how to make and keep friends. It includes numerous ideas for tough situations such as ways to settle an argument with a friend and how to handle bosses and bullies.

Brown, M. (1990). *Arthur's April fool.* Boston, MA: Little, Brown & Co.

Arthur's April Fool's surprise is almost spoiled by a bully.

Browne, A. (1989). *Willy the wimp.* New York: Knopf.

How to be gentle and kind without being a victim.

Browne, A. (1991). *Willy and Hugh.* New York: Knopf.

Burch, R. (2002). *Be a friend.* Huntington Beach, CA: Creative Teaching Press.

The positive character trait of learning about friendship and fairness is explored in this book.

Burnett, K. G. (1999). *Simon's hook.* Roseville, CA: GR Publishing. P.O. Box 1437, Roseville, CA 95678, or www.grandmarose.com.

Carlson, N. (1983). *Loudmouth George and the sixth grade bully.* New York: Puffin Books.

How George, with the help of his friend Harriet, thwarts an older and larger boy from stealing his lunch. How to support a victimized child through friendship is the theme of this story.

Carlson, N. (1988). *I like me.* New York: Viking.

An appealing little book about taking care of and valuing yourself. This book would be especially helpful for children who are victimized.

Carlson, N. (1997). *How to lose all your friends.* London: Puffin Books.

An easy-to-read picture book that teaches without preaching to young children about the importance of inter-personal skills. Readers experience why no one cares to play with a child who won't share, bullies, never smiles, and whines.

Cohen, M. (1987). *Liar, liar pants on fire.* New York: Young Yearling Books.

A boy who is new to his class tries to fit in by bragging.

Cole, J. (1989). *Bully Trouble.* New York: Random House.

Two friends team up to deal effectively with a bully.

The editors of Conari Press (1994). *Kids' random acts of kindness.* Berkeley, CA: Conari Press.

The refreshingly tender stories written by children remind the readers of the vital and joyful role that kindness can play in our lives.

Conta, M., & Reardon, M. (1974). *Feelings between friends.* Chicago, IL: Children's Press.

Fourteen photographically illustrated stories explore feelings and moods in relationships between children.

Crary, E. (1983). *My name is not dummy.* Seattle, WA: Parenting Press.

How to deal with put-downs.

Cummings, C. (1991). *Tattlin' Madeline.* Edmonds, WA: Teaching, Inc.

This excellent book helps children learn the difference between tattling and reporting.

Curtis, J.L., & Cornell, L. (2002). *I'm gonna like me: Letting off a little self-esteem.* New York: Joanna Cotler Books.

This adorable story highlights the point that the key to feeling good is liking yourself because you are you.

de Paola, T. (1979). *Oliver Button is a sissy.* New York: Harcourt Brace Jovanovich.

A young boy's coping with a put-down. This story builds empathy for being different and will help the caring majority understand.

DeRolf, S. (1996). *The crayon box that talked.* New York: Random House.

This is a simple story with an important message—working as a group produces wonderful results for all.

Doleski, T. (1983). *The hurt.* Mahwah, NJ: Paulist Press.

What happens to a young boy who hides his feelings and hurt.

Guffe, T. (1991). *Bully for you.* New York: Child's Play.

Why it's not a good idea to be a bully. A wonderful book for overly aggressive, young children tempted to bully others.

Hallinan, P.K. (1977). *That's what a friend is.* Nashville, TN: Ideals Children's Books.

This book reinforces the importance of both making friends and being a friend.

Heine, H. (1982). *Friends.* New York: Aladdin Paperbacks.

This story follows a group of animal friends through a typical day together. It emphasizes the importance of caring, sharing, and being fair because that is what good friends do. The illustrations and story are precious. This book is useful in defining friendship.

Henkes, K. (1988). *Chester's way.* New York: Mulberry Books.

The virtues of variety and friendship are beautifully handled in this amusing, believable story.

Henkes, K. (1991). *Chrysanthemum.* New York: Greenwillow Books.

A kindergarten-aged mouse is teased upon entering school because of her unusual name. The resolution is weak, but the story is engaging and builds empathy for the victim.

Hoffman, G. (1996). *The big bad bully bear.* New York: Random House.

A bully gets a second chance in this story.

Kellogg, S. (1990). *Best friends.* New York: Dial Books for Young Readers.

Many themes of friendship are covered in this wonderful story: creating fantasies to be accepted, loss of a friend, renewal of a friendship, as well as compromise and sharing.

Moser, A. (1988). *Don't pop your cork on Mondays.* Kansas City, MO: Landmark Editions.

Moser, A. (1991). *Don't feed the monster on Tuesday.* Kansas City, MO: Landmark Editions.

A wonderful book that presents valuable information to children about the importance of self-esteem. Practical approaches are presented that children can use to evaluate and strengthen their sense of self-esteem. A very practical guide to taking small steps toward success. Recommended for grades K–5, and definitely recommended for children who are victimized.

Moser, A. (1994). *Don't rant and rave on Wednesday*. Kansas City, MO: Landmark Editions.

Naylor, P.R. & Malone, N.L. (1994). *The king of the playground*. N.p.: Aladdin Paperbacks.

Kevin, with his dad's help and encouragement, learns how to overcome his fear of Sammy, the self-appointed "King of the Playground."

Payne, L.M. (1994). *Just because I am: A child's book of affirmation*. MN: Free Spirit Publishing, Inc.

This book shows children how to support and strengthen their self-esteem.

Payne, L.M. (1997). *We can get along: A child's book of choices*. MN: Free Spirit Publishing, Inc.

This book, for ages 3–8, is a warm and wonderful way to promote peaceful behaviors and positive conflict resolution.

Petty, K. & Firmin, C. (1991). *Being bullied*. New York: Barron's Books.

A young school-aged girl encounters a female bully who calls her names, teases, and scribbles on her papers. She tells her mom about her problem and she gets help from her teacher, who protects her from the bully.

Ross, D. (1999). *A book of friends*. New York: Harper Collins Publishers.

This sweet book explores the joys of friendship.

Walker, A. (1991). *Finding the greenstone*. San Diego, CA: Harcourt Brace Jovanovich.

A touching story about a boy finding compassion for others both from within himself and from the spirit of care given to him by his community. A strong book for helping the caring majority create a caring environment for all.

Wells, R. (1973). *Benjamin and Tulip*. New York: Dial Books.

A charming little animal story in which the bully is a girl and the victim is a boy. The situation resolves when they encounter a bigger problem that affects them both.

Wilt Berry, J. (1984). *Let's talk about fighting*. Chicago, IL: Children's Press.

A "self-help" book for young children that provides alternatives to fighting.

Zolotow, C. (1969). *The hating book*. New York: Harper Collins Children's Books.

A little girl knew her friend hated her but she didn't know why until she finally got up courage to ask why they were being so rotten to each other.

Zolotow, C. (1982). *The quarreling book*. New York: Harper Collins Children's Books.

A short story about how a quarrel can grow bigger and bigger until it hurts many people. For the youngest elementary children, this book builds an understanding of how aggression can spread unless stopped. A beginning guide to empower the caring majority.

Books for Intermediate Students

Adelman, B. & Hall, S. (1970). *On and off the street*. New York: Penguin USA.

Bennett, W.J. (Ed.) (1995). *The children's book of virtues*. New York: Simon & Schuster.

Classic stories, verses, poems, and fables are organized around different themes, each of which teaches a value. Courage, compassion, and honesty are just a few of the character values the book covers. It is short, easy to read, and a wonderful way to impart values through the timeless tradition of reading and storytelling.

Bosch, C. (1988). *Bully on the bus.* Seattle, WA: Parenting Press.

A terrific book that allows the reader to select from different options of how to handle a bully encountered on the school bus. For example, the victim can decide to fight back or to ask a friend for help by turning to different pages to learn the outcome. Children eventually read all the options, curious to find out which one proves the most effective. Many good ideas are presented for children who are victimized.

Burnett, K. G. (1999). *Simon's hook.* Roseville, CA: GR Publishing. P.O. Box 1437, Roseville, CA 95678, or www.grandmarose.com.

A book about teasing and put-downs, easily adapted to your child's situation and triggers. A real gem of a book.

▶ Byers, B. (1981). *The 18th emergency.* New York: Puffin Books.

CAUTION

A 12-year-old boy is tormented by the school bully for belittling him. His parents are of no help nor is his best friend, who is also frightened of the bully. Eventually he is beaten up by the bully.

Carrick, C. (1983). *What a wimp!* New York: Clarion Books.

Story of a fourth grade boy who moves to a new school following the divorce of his parents. He is harassed daily by a bully as he walks home from school. Finally, he decides to just let the bully beat him up. Surprisingly, the bully does nothing. The caring majority will understand what it feels like to be bullied after reading this book.

Cohen-Posey, K. (1995). *How to handle bullies, teasers, and other meanies.* Highland City, FL: Rainbow Books, Inc.

Why bullies and teasers act that way, how to deal with bullies and prejudice, and how to defend oneself against bullies.

Coombs, K. (1991). *Beating bully O'Brien.* New York: Avon Books.

A fifth grade boy is physically assaulted by a girl bully on his way home from school. His dad makes him feel like a sissy for not defending himself, but the boy is a viola player and he does not want to hurt his hands. When the bully's older brother attacks the boy, the girl bully intervenes and helps him. He later learns that she gets beaten up at home by her older brother. A good caring majority book as the main character is very likeable.

Estes, E. (1944). *The hundred dresses.* New York: Harcourt Brace Jovanovich.

A Newberry Honor story that will touch hearts. It is about the humiliation that results from teasing among elementary-aged girls. A good story to empower the caring majority.

Kaufman, G. & Raphael, L. (1990). *Stick up for yourself.* Minneapolis, MN: Free Spirit Publishing.

A guide to assertiveness and positive self-esteem. Discusses problems such as making choices, learning about and liking yourself, and solving problems. Recommended for grades 4–8. A wealth of ideas for children who are victimized.

Millman, D. (1991). *Secret of the peaceful warrior.* Tiburon, CA: H.J. Kramer.

An older mentor teaches a school-aged boy how to thwart a bully by hiding his fear and side-stepping his physical advances. Somewhat unrealistic, as the boy and the bully become friends in the end.

Naylor, P. (1991). *Reluctantly Alice.* New York: Atheneum.

> Story of a seventh grade girl who is made fun of in class, tripped in the halls, and hit by flying food in the cafeteria thrown by another girl and her cohorts. When each student in class must select someone to interview, the girl chooses the bully. The girls eventually come to know each other better and the bullying stops.

Pfeffer, S.B. (1979). *Awful Evelina.* Morton Grove, IL: Albert Whitman.

Rochman, H. & McCampbell, D. (1993). *Who do you think you are? Stories of friends and enemies.* Boston, MA: Little, Brown, & Co.

> A collection of short stories about friendship—being a friend, being let down, being picked on, and being cared about. A great book for enlisting the empathy of the caring majority.

Romain, T. (1997). *Bullies are a pain in the brain.* Minneapolis, MN: Free Spirit Publishing, Inc.

> This handbook approach offers children tried-and-true ways to deal with bullies as they laugh along with the author's jokes and cartoons. This book also provides help to kids who are bullies and want to change.

CAUTION ▶ Stolz, M. (1963). *The bully of Barkham Street.* New York: Harper Collins Children's Books.

> The main character in this story is the bully. He is a sixth grade boy who is the oldest and biggest in his classroom. His family rarely listens to him and often threatens to take away his only friend, his dog.

Wood, W. & Wood, A. (1975). *The sandwich.* Toronto, Canada: Kids Can Press.

> A wonderful story that employs humor and cleverness in solving a situation of being made fun of because of ethnicity. This book shows how to support the victim.